COLLINS

Literacy at 11–14

A practical guide to raising achievement through whole-school literacy development

**Julia Strong
Deputy Director,
National Literacy Trust**

Collins Educational

An imprint of HarperCollinsPublishers

**NATIONAL
LITERACY
TRUST**

Building a literate nation

Published by Collins Educational
77-85 Fulham Palace Road, London W6 8JB
An imprint of HarperCollinsPublishers

The HarperCollins website address is: www.**fire**and**water**.com

First Published 1999
Reprinted 1999 (twice).

ISBN 000 323 080 5

British Library Cataloguing in Publication Data
A cataloguing record for this book is available from the British Library

Author's Acknowledgements
The ideas within this handbook have been greatly influenced by all who contributed to the success of the National Literacy Trust training conferences on whole-school approaches to literacy in 1997, 1998 and 1999, in particular Margaret Meek, Peter Traves, Elizabeth Plackett and John Hertrich. They have all been, like myself, greatly influenced in the development of their ideas by the best practice they have seen in hundreds of schools over the years.
The philosophy of this handbook reflects that of the National Literacy Trust, which believes in building partnerships and networks to improve literacy standards. The impetus behind this book is to recognise that the development of good practice is based on the sharing of effective ideas.

Dedication
To anyone who ever recommended a good book to me, especially my brother Phil.

Acknowledgements
The editor and publisher would like to thank those concerned for permission
to reproduce extracts from the following material:

The Cheshire Cat's Guide to Grammar by George Keith, Cheshire Advisory and Inspection Service (page 44); Televizyon: Olduren Eglence, translation of Amusing Ourselves to Death, by Neil Postman, Ayrinti Yayinlari, 1994 (page 52); Extending Literacy – children reading and writing non-fiction, by David Wray and Maureen Lewis, Routledge, 1997 (pages 54, 59, 60, 64) ; Reads like a novel, by Daniel Pennac, Quartet Books Ltd, 1994 (page 58); 'Joy when the maths adds up', The Times Educational Supplement July 1990, © Times Supplements Limited, 1998 (page 76); EXEL Writing Frames, by David Wray and Maureen Lewis, National Literacy Trust (pages 84–85); advertisement for Hermesetas, Hermes Sweetners(page 108); quotation from Gena Merrett (page 118); quotation from Alan Tuckett (page 118); Fever Pitch by Nick Hornby, Victor Gollancz Ltd (page 131); Left Foot in the Grave by Gary Nelson and Anthony Fowles, HarperCollins Publishers Ltd (page 133); 'The Roy'sDone Good', Daily Mirror 10th December 1998, Mirror Syndication International (page 135); Appendix 1 Useful HMI Checklists, OFSTED (pages 119–121).

Commissioned by Helen Clark
Project management by Helen Clark
Edited by Lucy Hobbs, Jo Kemp
Cover design by Nigel Jordan
Internal design by Jenny Fleet
Cover photograph by Telegraph Colour Library
Production by Susan Cashin
Printed and bound by Martins the Printers, Berwick-upon-Tweed

Contents

About the National Literacy Trust

The National Literacy Trust is a charity established in 1993 to work in partnership with others to enhance literacy standards throughout the United Kingdom.

The Trust's purpose is to make an independent strategic contribution to the creation of a society in which all can enjoy the appropriate skills, confidence and pleasures of literacy to support their educational, economic, social and cultural goals. The Trust promotes a systemic partnership-based approach to building a literate nation.

In order to help achieve this aim the Trust:

☐ maintains an on-line database and provides information and support to all those interested in enhancing literacy standards
☐ contributes to national and local policy and practice
☐ publishes *Literacy Today* – a cross-sector snapshot of effective approaches to teaching literacy
☐ promotes and facilitates literacy partnership networks
☐ organises courses, seminars and conferences
☐ runs 'Reading Is Fundamental, UK' – creating a new generation of readers by providing motivating events and free books for children
☐ encourages and supports the involvement of the business sector
☐ is continuing the National Year of Reading: Read on: National Reading Campaign
☐ and will be continuing the partnership approach of the Year with the launch of an annual conference 'Partnerships for Literacy', promoting a systemic approach to building literate communities.

National Literacy Trust
Swire House
59 Buckingham Gate
London, SW1 6AJ

 Tel: 0171 828 2435
 Fax: 0171 931 9986

 Email: contact@literacytrust.org.uk
 Website: www.literacytrust.org.uk

Acronyms and abbreviations used in this book

BECTa	British Educational Communications and Technology agency
BSA	Basic Skills Agency
DARTs	Directed Activities Related to Texts
DENI	Department of Education for Northern Ireland
DfEE	Department for Education and Employment
EAL	English as an Additional Language
Estyn	The school inspectorate in Wales - it means to reach in Welsh
EXEL	Exeter Extending Literacy project
GCSE	General Certificate of Secondary Education
HE	Higher Education
HMI	Her Majesty's Inspectorate
IEP	Individual Education Plans
ICT	Information and Communication Technology
ILS	Integrated Learning Systems
INSET	In-service training
IT	Information Technology
KS1/2/3/4	Key Stage 1/2/3/4
KWL grids	What do I Know? What do I Want to know? What have I learnt? Grids
LEA	Local Education Authority
OFSTED	Office For Standards in Education
QCA	Qualifications and Curriculum Authority (formerly known as SCAA)
NAAE	National Association of Advisers in English
NFER	National Foundation for Educational Research
NLS	National Literacy Strategy
NYR	National Year of Reading
SATs	Standard Assessment Tests (Note this is a colloquial term used by teachers and the media to refer to the National Curriculum tests. It is not their official name because SATS is the registered trade name for specific tests set America.)
SEN	Special Educational Needs
SENCO	Special Educational Needs Co-ordinator
TES	Times Educational Supplement

Introduction

Approach

The present emphasis on building an effective whole-school approach to literacy is an excellent opportunity for every school with students aged 11–14 to improve the quality of classroom practice in every curriculum area, alongside raising the literacy standards of all students. This has the potential to be a really significant initiative with long-lasting positive effects for both children and teachers, rather than another bureaucratic, ill-thought-through scheme that quietly fizzles out after months of effort by those attempting to make it work.

This book is based on the premise that there is already excellent practice in many departments of every school that is not sufficiently shared. Its purpose is to suggest ways of developing literacy across the curriculum, centred on improving classroom practice through working in partnership within the school and beyond. There is much scope here for truly effective change that builds professional collaboration. At its best it can 'create a climate of confidence in which innovation can take place' (spokesperson for the Newham Key Stage 3 project).

Literacy at 11–14 is a practical guide to developing an approach to literacy across the curriculum that will underpin teaching in every subject area. It is not about doing the English or SEN department's job, but about improving the use of language in every area, be it spoken, read or written. It is full of references and practical examples from a wide range of curriculum areas, with a grid to show which suggestions are best suited to each subject. It provides an overview of a whole-school literacy policy, with material for any literacy working party to consider on the structure, targets, monitoring, evaluation and development of the policy, as well as practical proposals for improving classroom practice.

A do-it-yourself guide to in-service literacy training

This book's focus is a series of suggested handouts and OHP slides with accompanying background information and presenter' notes, which could form the basis of interactive in-service training, plus follow-up planning and training. Alternatively, the suggested training can be broken up into a series of shorter sessions to be conducted within a focus group or specific curriculum area and built up over time. The sections can also stand alone so that individuals wishing to train themselves on how to integrate literacy into their method of teaching can use the handbook for this purpose.

All aspects of this training will need to be developed if an effective whole-school approach to literacy is to be established. How this development might take place is suggested in the commentary that accompanies the handouts. The book concludes with ways to develop the ideas begun by the training into an effective policy rooted in improving classroom practice, recognising the contribution that can be made to the development of literacy by all curriculum areas. The people who have been involved in developing these ideas concur that there can be no quick fix. Staff development days, meetings and writing the policy are only the starting point.

The structure of the book

Background information and suggestions for future action introduce ready-to-run materials that are labelled to indicate one of the following functions:

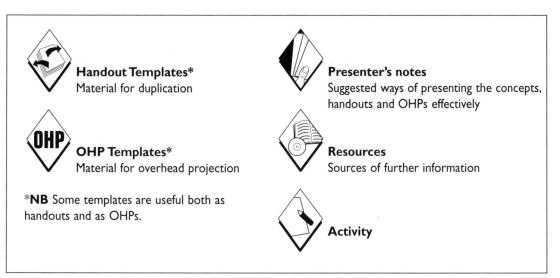

Handout Templates*
Material for duplication

Presenter's notes
Suggested ways of presenting the concepts, handouts and OHPs effectively

OHP Templates*
Material for overhead projection

Resources
Sources of further information

***NB** Some templates are useful both as handouts and as OHPs.

Activity

Literacy across the UK

This book is relevant to middle and secondary schools throughout the UK. However, writing about school education in a way that communicates to readers throughout the UK, can be tricky. The national press tends to write as if every utterance of the DfEE were statutory throughout the UK. But the Department for Education and Employment deals with education in England only; in Wales, its equivalent is the Education Department within the Welsh Office; in Scotland it is The Scottish Office Education and Industry Department, and in Northern Ireland it is the Department of Education for Northern Ireland (DENI). Each of these departments has a different approach to education and therefore may use different terminology to describe the various age groups and sectors; this is particularly so in Scotland.

In order to avoid endless unwieldy alternative terminology in brackets, this text will use the terminology of the English curriculum, since this is largely used in Wales and Northern Ireland, while providing the chart below to show alternative terminology used in other parts of the UK. For similar reasons of brevity, from this point onward, the term secondary school will be used to cover all schools teaching children aged between 11 and 14, whether they be secondary, middle or special.

Age	England and Wales	Northern Ireland	Scotland
4–5	KSI YrR	KSI PI	Primary I
5–6	Yr1	P2	P2
6–7	Yr2	P3	P3
7–8	KS2 Yr3	KS2 P4	P4
8–9	Yr4	P5	P5
9–10	Yr5	P6	P6
10–11	Yr6	P7	P7
11–12	KS3 Yr7	KS3 Yr8	Secondary I
12–13	Yr8	Yr9	S2
13–14	Yr9	Yr10	S3
14–15	KS4 Yr10	Yr11	S4
15–16	Yr11	Yr12	S5
16–17	KS5 Yr12 (L6)	Yr13 (L6)	S6
17–18	Yr13 (U6)	Yr14 (U6)	

Scotland

Education in Scotland has been organised separately from that in England and Wales since the Act of Union of 1707. Education is among the powers delegated to the Scottish Parliament.

There is no national curriculum in Scotland. The national guidelines in the 5–14 programme are based on reports of working parties of professionals closely linked to work in the schools. Assessment policy is significantly different from that in England. National testing has been established to monitor progress but teachers decide when, during a child's primary school career, is the appropriate time to give the national tests. There are no league tables based on national testing. There is also more emphasis on the centrality of the teacher in assessing and monitoring progress. This is reflected in the Scottish HMI inspection system.

Resource
A useful book outlining the key differences between the Scottish and English approaches to education is *Education in Scotland: Policy and practice from pre-school to secondary*, edited by Margaret M Clark and Pamela Munn (Routledge).

Wales
There is a separate Welsh Inspectorate (recently renamed ESTYN, Welsh for to reach or to stretch) but it is run on the same lines as OFSTED. There are no primary school league tables and a separate curriculum accommodates Welsh language teaching into secondary schools. Welsh primary schools are not expected to teach the literacy hour, which is a matter for 'local discretion'. Teachers have been told that they may choose whatever strategies they deem fit, and heads instructed that there is no one way to teach literacy successfully. Every Welsh local authority must draw up a strategy on literacy, based on good practice from the best schools. Individual schools must set and monitor their own targets. Control of education has been delegated from the Welsh Office to the Welsh Assembly.

Northern Ireland
Northern Ireland's general approach to education is fairly similar to that followed by the DfEE, the major exception being that it retained the 11+, with the related grammar school system, for 40% of children; the other 60% go to secondary highs. Most of the schools are denominational and many are single sex. The National Curriculum is divided into the same four Key Stages as in England, with their related programmes of study, attainment targets and level descriptions, but there are six curriculum areas of study as opposed to England's ten.

Like Wales, DENI decided not to adopt England's literacy hour approach in the primary sector. The recent School Improvement Programme has asked schools to focus on literacy, numeracy and ICT. All secondary schools were required to have literacy co-ordinators from September 1998. The literacy target for 11-year-olds by the year 2002 is the same as England's (80% of students performing at level 4). However, targets for Key Stage 3 have also been introduced that are differentiated to reflect the selective nature of the system. Thus, by the year 2002, 100% of grammar school students are expected to be achieving at level 5 or above in English; 60% of students in secondary highs are expected to be achieving at this level.

Resource
Northern Ireland's approach is explained in *A Strategy for the Promotion of Literacy and Numeracy in Northern Ireland*, which is summarised on the NLT website (www.literacytrust.org.uk/Update/ireland.html).

England's focus on literacy

The DfEE in England has the most developed approach to literacy across the curriculum. This will doubtless be looked at with varied levels of interest by the rest of the UK. However, there is a UK-wide movement towards raising literacy standards through involving all teachers. For example, all secondary schools in Northern Ireland were required to have literacy co-ordinators from September 1998. In Wales, the Welsh Education White Paper of July 1997 recognised that a sustained focus on effective methods of teaching literacy was necessary for all students in both primary and secondary schools. Wales, like England, began by focusing on the former.

In England the DfEE's National Literacy Strategy contained only a brief reference to the secondary sector in the initial document when it was published in September 1997. This is summarised by the following paragraph:

'Every secondary school should specialise in literacy and set targets for improvement in English. Similarly every teacher should contribute to promoting it. The principles for the management of literacy set out earlier apply as much to secondary schools as to primary schools. In shaping their plans it is essential that secondary schools do not see reading and writing as exclusively the province of a few teachers in the English and learning support departments.'

(Paragraph 112)

In the academic year 1998–1999 the DfEE funded 22 pilot schemes in LEAs in England to develop strategies to tackle low literacy standards in the first years of secondary school. Pilot projects included:

☐ Extending the National Literacy Framework to Key Stage 3
☐ Adapting the literacy hour to Year 7
☐ Exploring the culture of the school as a literate community
☐ Improving/developing effective catch-up programmes
☐ Providing literacy training for secondary teachers.

The DfEE perspective

The following quotation sums up the centrality of language across the curriculum to the DfEE's approach:

'The National Literacy Strategy recognises that literacy cannot be learnt in isolation. Reading and writing are essential across the curriculum. It is therefore important that the co-ordination of literacy planning, teaching and assessment is treated as a whole school issue. This commitment is seen as essential for all students whether or not they have been taking part in a summer literacy school, or are entering a Key Stage 3 intervention programme.'

(extract from NLS planning materials for Key Stage 3, March 1999)

Expectations for 1999–2000

There are two parts to the DfEE's extension of the National Literacy Strategy to Key Stage 3 for 1999–2000:

☐ Schools are expected to be moving towards a whole-school approach to literacy, including an intervention programme
☐ The summer literacy schools are to be linked to Key Stage 3 intervention programmes.

In June 1999 three key members of staff from every state school in England that includes Year 7 students, were expected to attend a two-day conference on the extension of the National Literacy Strategy to Key Stage 3. There were some very useful materials for schools to support these training days (see page 141 under Government Publications).

Following this training, all schools with Key Stage 3 students are expected to be moving towards a whole-school approach to literacy. This should include a programme to help ensure that all students who are below the level expected for their age in English make progress towards having the literacy skills commensurate with their age. There is a significant emphasis on an intervention programme related to the primary framework, but this is not the exclusive focus. For the academic year 1999–2000 there is no specific detailed framework for the teaching of literacy in secondary schools, but schools are expected to build on the primary framework.

Longer-term expectations

Clearly the above is less prescriptive than the National Literacy Strategy is for the primary sector. The primary literacy hour is based on the National Literacy Project that was piloted from 1996 before being implemented in 1998. However, the impact of the 1998–1999 Key Stage 3 pilot projects is still being evaluated. There is not sufficient evidence yet from these to say that secondary schools should follow one specific route. It may be that for ensuing years, following the proper evaluation of the projects, there will be more precise targets and programmes of work for secondary schools in England.

Working together to get it right

Given this timescale, schools are in an excellent position to develop an approach that really works and which stimulates the sharing of good practice. This can be achieved by setting up a training programme based on developing and learning from the best practice that already exists within schools, aided by the experience of LEA literacy advisers.

Stop press

Just as this book was going to press in late July, the following information was received from the Qualifications and Curriculum Authority.

In England, there will *not* be an extension of the present Key Stages 1 and 2 NLS literacy framework for Key Stage 3. However, in line with the approach suggested in this book, all secondary schools will be expected to have the following three elements in place:

☐ an intervention programme for students who transfer to secondary school with literacy skills below their chronological age
☐ a literacy component that is taught within the English curriculum
☐ a whole-school approach to literacy that sees literacy as an integral part of the curriculum planning of all subject areas.

The QCA is in the process of developing exemplar schemes of work for all subject areas to help schools implement the new subject orders at Key Stage 3. Each unit will include at least one literacy objective based on a coherent set of literacy expectations for students across all subjects. These exemplars and related literacy expectations will go out to consultation in September and should be published in April 2000.

How to start your school thinking about literacy

Defining policy

Throughout this book, the word 'policy' is used according to the definition of Peter Traves, headteacher, Wakeman School, Shropshire: 'Policy is an agreed set of practices that underpin what a school does, and that are to be acted on and monitored.' A good litmus test of a policy is whether a teacher who has joined the school since it was drafted both knows of the policy and implements it.

The Bullock Report *(A Language for Life)* emphasised the need for a coherent language policy in every school:
'Every school should have an organised policy for language across the curriculum establishing every teacher's involvement in language and reading development throughout the years of schooling.'

(Report of the Bullock Committee Inquiry, 1974, principal recommendation no 4)

But somehow the process lost direction. In the words of John Hertrich, HMI, 'The key difference between now and the Bullock era is that the current attention to language and literacy practices focuses much more on methods of teaching'. This book is concerned with putting the good ideas that lay behind the Bullock Report into effective practice. The key issue is not a complex compiling of literacy entitlement, but rather, what is being done to make this entitlement a reality. What is needed is an approach built around a programme of in-service training that is focused on developing quality teaching: one that underpins how all staff plan their lessons.

Defining literacy

Some people suggest that defining literacy is the necessary starting point. This discussion carries a health warning. Defining literacy has much in common with defining time, as summed up by St Augustine some 1,500 years ago: 'If nobody asks me, I know what time is. But if I am asked to define it, I do not know'. You can spend a very long and heated time debating a definition of literacy and finally arrive at a convoluted statement. The process may take hours of meeting time and leave the majority even more convinced that meetings are a waste of time. However, some sort of working definition is necessary. Perhaps the best time to finalise your school's definition of literacy is once work on your whole-school approach is well under way. Staff will then be in a position to consider its implications in practice. Schools may find the one below from the HMI secondary literacy survey a useful starting point:
'Literacy can be defined on a number of levels. It is obviously concerned with the ability to read and write but a fuller definition might be the capacity to recognise, reproduce and manipulate the conventions of text shared by a given community'.

(A summary of this useful survey is available in Appendix I, page 119)

In the same document it is stated that:
'Literacy is not something separate from English. It is a vital subset of English and it is also an aspect of our communicative abilities. It cannot be separated entirely from oracy, on which it builds, and it is an essential part of the learning process. Literacy is, or ought to be, a shared responsibility – it is too important to leave to English teachers... There are new forms of literacy (on-screen literacy and moving image media) to consider alongside the more traditional print literacy. Literacy is important because it enables pupils to gain access to the subjects studied in school, to read for information and pleasure, and to communicate effectively. Poor levels of literacy impact negatively on what pupils can do and how they see themselves.'

Some schools may prefer to use the term 'language' instead of 'literacy'.

It is also worth remembering that the HMI survey identified the following recognition as a central feature of successful practice:
'The school sees literacy as the key to improving learning and raising standards and has an approach which is relevant to all curriculum areas and pupils of all levels of attainment.'

(all three quotations above from *Secondary Literacy: A survey by HMI* by John Hertrich, HMI)

Presenter's notes

The above quotations are been reproduced as Template 1, page 9, for use with staff training.

South Camden Community School's definition of a literate person is *'one who has the ability to process information critically through interaction of their knowledge of the world and the information that is presented in writing and other media.'*

One way of finalising your school's definition of literacy is to consider the HMI definitions on Template 1, page 9 alongside the definition above. Using this material as a starting point, each curriculum area group could be given half an hour to come up with its own definition of literacy, plus any supporting arguments the group may wish to proffer. Each version could then be considered by the literacy co-ordinator who could present a proposal to the working party and then to the whole staff. This process involves everyone, but it avoids the pitfall of trying to finalise your definition in committee.

‘*Literacy can be defined on a number of levels. It is obviously concerned with the ability to read and write but a fuller definition might be the capacity to recognise, reproduce and manipulate the conventions of text shared by a given community.*’

‘*Literacy is not something separate from English. It is a vital subset of English and it is also an aspect of our communicative abilities. It cannot be separated entirely from oracy, on which it builds, and it is an essential part of the learning process. Literacy is, or ought to be, a shared responsibility – it is too important to leave to English teachers... There are new forms of literacy (on-screen literacy and moving image media) to consider alongside the more traditional print literacy. Literacy is important because it enables pupils to gain access to the subjects studied in school, to read for information and pleasure, and to communicate effectively. Poor levels of literacy impact negatively on what pupils can do and how they see themselves.*’

The following has been identified as a central feature of successful practice:

‘*The school sees literacy as the key to improving learning and raising standards and has an approach which is relevant to all curriculum areas and pupils of all levels of attainment.*’

(all three quotations from *Secondary Literacy: A survey by HMI* by John Hertrich, HMI)

Key issues

The first thing that needs to be done is to set up a structure and timescale within which teachers can work effectively. The structure and timescale must then be reflected in the school development plan. This section tackles issues that must be addressed when setting up such a system. You may wish to introduce this in your staff training programme in order to involve the staff in the full process, but the issues raised here will need significant consideration by any literacy working party and will all require fresh consideration on a regular basis. The following five areas demand particular attention:

☐ Leadership
☐ Timing
☐ Reviewing the literacy curriculum
☐ Targets, monitoring and evaluation
☐ Implications for timing, training, resources and school organisation.

Leadership

Central to structure is the question of leadership. It is advisable to set up some sort of literacy working party to provide and maintain momentum. The composition of such a working party is crucial. It would be best to ensure that this group includes at least one member of the senior management team who is determined to move the issue forward, plus a representative of each curriculum area to reach out to all teaching staff. (Including all areas may make the working party unwieldy in size, but if you leave areas out you will need a plan to incorporate all areas over time.) It might be best to try to get enthusiastic volunteers to represent each curriculum area, rather than necessarily rounding up the heads of areas. If the head of a curriculum area lacks enthusiasm on this issue, they will lack the will to feed back and involve their area appropriately in this initiative. It may be best not to have the Head of English or SENCO leading the working party, as this can compound other curriculum areas' possible belief that the issue doesn't really concern their area. However, some schools' policies are very well led by the Head of English or SEN. Some schools have begun successfully with small working parties involving a few key curriculum areas. The staff involved have then developed the approach in their areas and helped to prepare the training for all staff.

If your working party does not gel and create an exhilarating group, it is bound to limit the effectiveness of the initiative. It is worthwhile considering how you will ensure positive representation from the following:

☐ An effective member of the senior management team with the drive and ability to get things done
☐ Enthusiastic representatives from several, though not necessarily all, curriculum areas, but definitely including English, SEN and the librarian.

Additional options:

☐ Consider setting up a core team consisting of some combination of senior manager, literacy co-ordinator, Head of English and SENCO, who could meet more frequently and steer the group
☐ Consider giving a small minority of working party places (perhaps two) to representatives from curriculum areas that are resisting the initiative, to attempt to move them forward
☐ Consider focusing exclusively on reading across the curriculum (see Template 9, page 24 for an illustration of this approach).

Timing

This issue comes with the most serious health warning of any in this book. Don't be pressurised into doing too much, too quickly. It is better to do a few things well, and build staff confidence and belief in the approach, than to attempt too much, achieve nothing well and undermine the possibility of future success. This is a long-term strategy that needs to be built on firm foundations. Timing the development of your policy could be tricky. Everyone with long experience of developing whole-school approaches to literacy seems to agree that it is a mistake to try to achieve too much, too fast, and suggests selecting the timescale appropriate to your school. But, at the same time, the political imperative driving the Government's National Literacy Strategy means that for secondary schools in England the pressure is on for some to sprint before they can walk.

Schools that run a Summer Literacy Programme are expected to meet all the points outlined on page 33. These may be achievable if your school is already part of a related Key Stage 3 pilot project and thus has specific staff who are already very familiar with planning and teaching within the framework of the literacy hour. But many of the 900 schools taking part were not in this position and will need to assess realistically what they can achieve. Equally, some schools are perhaps two years down the road of building a whole-school approach to literacy and have, under their own initiative, taken the time to see how the literacy hour works in primary schools; teaching within the English/SEN departments has been adapted to build on this framework.

Each school will be starting from a different position. The best way to devise your timetable is to assess honestly where you are starting from. From that base point, devise the timescale and targets for development that are realistic for your school, rather than desperately trying to achieve all the points on the Key Stage 3 check-list in one fell swoop. A realistic schedule should have tangible, ambitious, yet achievable targets, and an evaluation system clearly related to these targets. To be successful, the literacy policy needs to be built into the structure and practice of the school; changing structures and practice takes time.

A good place to start would be to take a long and sober look at the lists of things to be done by schools in the summer literacy programme (page 33) and then to ask the questions on the following checklist.

Where are we now? Checklist

■ Are key staff already familiar enough with the teaching style and framework of the literacy hour to be able to plan and teach effectively in this mode?

■ Do all staff consider the literacy aspects of what is to be taught when planning and delivering units of work?

■ Is the importance of reading visible around the school?

■ Is there an effective, focused intervention programme for pupils with literacy difficulties?

Having considered these questions honestly, ask the following simple question. What, realistically, can we manage successfully in the next year? Then plan accordingly.

On page 33 there is a list of the elements that schools are supposed to include in their Key Stage 3 intervention programme. The fifth point here, 'organise staff training', refers to providing 'guidance for subject teachers on how they can support students' literacy development across the curriculum'. Just pause to consider what this actually means. If it is to have any meaning in practice, it would involve setting up a programme of training for all staff on integrating literacy into their lesson planning. To change practice in the classroom would involve a programme that would take at least a year.

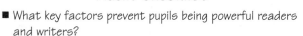

Presenter's notes

Template 2, page 13 is a possible timescale for building an effective whole-school approach to literacy, based on a training programme to improve and share good classroom practice. This is a model way forward for schools just starting to develop this approach. Of course, it will need to be adjusted depending on your school's present state of development. The working party could then use the template to consider the following issues.

Timing

- Is it a reasonable timescale given your school's situation? If not, what amendments are proposed?
- The template offers a more detailed timescale for involving all curriculum areas. What timetable is the working party proposing for the other strands listed under the heading 'Working party decides timescale for...'
- It is worth considering at this point that there are three main strands to a whole-school approach to literacy:
  - Creating a reading ethos
  - Ensuring there is an effective intervention programme
  - Involving all curriculum areas.

  Do you want to focus on all three areas concurrently, or spread them out over time?

Leadership

- Are all three strands outlined above to be headed up by the literacy co-ordinator and overseen by the working party?
- Are there going to be two subgroups: one to oversee creating a reading ethos; the other the intervention programme?
- When and how will the working party feed back information to the heads of areas and whole staff?
- How are the governors to be involved?

Training

- Is the proposed training programme on the draft timetable appropriate for your school? If not, what amendments do you want?
- How are you going to ensure that sufficient training time is going to be allocated to this issue both from INSET days and departmental and school meeting time?
- Who will deliver the initial INSET?
- Which curriculum areas do you think will be in the best position to lead the follow-up training day?

Resources

What resources are available and what is needed to make this initiative successful?
The working party may wish to consider the necessity for and resource implications of the following:

- Prioritising two training days for literacy in the coming year, with a view to improving classroom practice
- Allowing non-teaching time in the following year's timetable to enable heads of curriculum areas both to monitor

classroom practice in relation to literacy and to facilitate a programme where teachers have some opportunity to see others teach.

- Providing all staff, or groups of staff, with training on grammar
- Providing training for SEN staff on a focused intervention programme
- Providing training for English and SEN staff on the literacy hour
- Providing Year 7 tutors with texts for a reading programme in registration time.

School organisation

- What changes will be necessary to the school timetable to provide a focused intervention programme for Year 7 students who have difficulties with literacy?
- How will the working party ensure that literacy becomes embedded within departmental curriculum planning?
- How will the school development plan be altered to ensure that literacy is a priority when planning.
- How will this initiative be embedded within the school? (You may wish to consider page 100 here.)

Reviewing the literacy curriculum: whole-school literacy audits

A useful starting point is to establish what literacy practice there is in each department. One way of reviewing the literacy curriculum is via a whole-school audit. Below are four important factors to consider during the course of this audit:

Audit checklist

- What key factors prevent pupils being powerful readers and writers?
- What are the literacy requirements and practices of each subject area?
- What texts do departments use and what do they do with them?
- Looking at a range of exercise books can be useful for establishing the range of written tasks being set.

There are several possible approaches to carrying out such an audit, including:

Questionnaires Send a questionnaire to all curriculum areas to discover what each sees as the literacy requirements of their area and what literacy practices are in place

Observation A member of staff observes a selection of lessons to see what the literacy content of lessons is in practice

Sampling work Members of the working party look at the exercise books of a sample of children.

Clearly there are drawbacks to each method. The questionnaires may reflect ideals or wishful thinking more than reality. If staff know their literacy practices are being observed, they may alter their lessons accordingly. Looking at exercise books is a good way of seeing what written tasks were set and how they were carried out, but they will not record the text input or oral aspects of lessons. However, despite the potential in-built bias of at least the first two processes, which could lead to audits presenting an optimistic picture, the outcomes of such literacy audits tend to be very sobering.

Below are the typical findings of school literacy audits, not as carried out by inspectors, but by the school. Are these findings applicable to your school?

Typical literacy audit findings checklist

- Lots of copying.
- Much unchallenging comprehension work.
- Pupils encounter a minimal range of texts.
- Reading is often restricted to short bursts of a few seconds.
- Writing usually consists of very short unfinished pieces.
- Pupils are not taught how to use reference materials.
- Widespread use of (often ill-designed) worksheets.
- Insufficient opportunities for oral work.
- Good practice that is not shared.

Presenter's notes
These findings are reproduced in handout form on Template 24, page 50. They are a useful way of introducing staff to the need to consider literacy practices within their area. See Appendix 2, page 122, for an example of how one school set about an audit and what it discovered.

Resources
The KS3 Literacy Conferences Video contains interesting reflections by teachers and literacy advisers on the usefulness of literacy audits in raising staff awareness. Schools will find their local literacy advisers can also offer much help with literacy audits.

Targets, monitoring and evaluation

A central task for the working party will be setting appropriate targets, then monitoring and evaluating them. However, it is vital to start by considering what you are actually going to do that will be measured in these ways. There is a danger that evaluation will concentrate on things that are easily measured objectively, such as reading ages, whereas qualities like enthusiasm get neglected because they are hard to measure objectively.

Presenter's notes
A timely reminder in relation to this is the quotation from the Leverhulme Project on Template 3, page 14 which you may wish to use for discussion and/or training on targets and evaluation.

It is important to set up an evaluation process that values and encourages exchange of good practice and self-evaluation. Since classroom practice is at the heart of the policy, if possible, set up a system that allows teachers to observe and exchange best practice within and beyond their curriculum areas.

Presenter's notes
Your policy will need appropriate targets that in turn must be monitored and evaluated. On Template 4, page 15 are lists of questions and possible areas for targets. Before attempting to set any targets, it is worth reminding the working party, if not the whole staff, of what constitutes a useful target.

Template 5, page 16, on SMART targets is a useful discussion activity to help to achieve this. It could form part of tutor training on setting and monitoring effective literacy-related targets for students.

Draft timescale for beginning to develop your whole-school approach

This is a possible timescale for building an effective whole-school approach to literacy. It is a model for schools just starting to develop this approach, but, it could be adapted to suit schools at different stages of development.

Target timescale	Action
Early autumn term (e.g. September 1999)	Appoint Literacy Co-ordinator
Early autumn term (e.g. September 1999)	Set up literacy working party, including a representative from the senior management team, the Literacy Co-ordinator, enthusiasts from a broad spread of curriculum areas, plus key representatives from English and SEN.
Early autumn term (e.g. October 1999)	Working party decides timescale for: ☐ Literacy audit ☐ Initial strategy, targets, monitoring and evaluation of policy agreed ☐ Reading ethos developed ☐ Intervention strategy reviewed ☐ English and SEN teachers trained in literacy hour approach ☐ Tutors involved in reading ethos and target setting ☐ All curriculum areas involved in literacy development.

The following more detailed timescale focuses exclusively on the last point, namely, involving all curriculum areas.

Target timescale	Action
Late November 1999–January 2000	Whole-school training day adapted from that outlined in this book (see Template 6, page 18) to get ideas off the ground.
Spring term (2000)	Inter-departmental discussion to agree: ☐ Whole-school approach to marking ☐ Timetable for introduction of aspects of whole-school approach to literacy, including targets for pupils and curriculum areas.
Early summer term (2000)	Second training day on literacy/classroom practice, focusing on giving departments/curriculum areas the workshop time to develop further the ideas presented in the first training day. This day could be introduced by a range of departments, focusing on different aspects of the suggestions from the previous training day and showing how these can be adapted for areas to enrich the quality of lessons. For example: ☐ **Maths:** word/concept games and modelling the thinking process ☐ **Science:** thinking frames and writing frames ☐ **Drama:** controlling and developing oral group activities ☐ **Geography:** DARTs activities, including modelling reading.
Mid-summer term (2000)	Interdepartmental meeting to agree timetable for all curriculum areas to have included literacy targets and related processes within their curriculum planning for all year groups, beginning with Year 7 (progress to be reported to governors).
September (2000)	☐ All departments including literacy targets within the Year 7 curriculum planning. ☐ Pupil literacy targets in place. ☐ Meeting for parents of new intake to involve them in literacy programme. ☐ Whole-school approach to marking to be implemented by all areas for all years. ☐ Literacy to be visible around the school, including departmental plans to achieve this. ☐ A series of additional literacy targets agreed, including a timescale for inclusion of literacy targets for all years.
First day back, September 2000 (part of INSET day)	English department outlines Year 7 unit of work that builds on the structure, content, focus and processes underlying the literacy hour, so that all curriculum areas can help build on common ground.
Autumn term 2000	Programme allowing some teachers to observe other teachers teaching is initiated.
Autumn term 2000	Ongoing programme for induction of new staff into the process.
Academic year 2000–2001	☐ Ongoing programme for sharing of expertise. ☐ Ongoing programme to achieve, monitor and evaluate literacy targets and adapt policy.

David

At the beginning of Year 5 David was adamant: *'I absolutely hate reading. It's boring. I just don't like it.'*

Only his Liverpool comic was of any interest. No one read to him at home and he was a seasoned procrastinator in class, able to turn finding a pencil into a five-minute task.

By the following June he was transformed. *'Reading? I like it,'* he said.

Asked why the change of heart, he was equally unambiguous: *'It's Mrs Jackson. She's given me some really good books, adventures and that sort of stuff, and books that made me laugh.'*

Patrick Burson's *The Funfair of Evil* had been particularly enjoyed. Mrs Jackson's personalised approach increased the time and effort he spent on reading. Although his test score had only improved slightly, his attitude and the number and range of books he read had soared.

(from the Leverhulme-funded Primary Improvement *Project Raising Literacy Standards: From Policy to Practice* – a paper presented at the Annual Conference of the British Educational Research Association, September 1996, by E.C. Wragg, C.M. Wragg, G.S. Haynes and R. Chamberlain)

Developing policy

Aspects of policy requiring targets to be monitored and evaluated

- Structure and systems
- Creating a reading ethos
- Departmental practice
- Monitoring overall pupil progress
- Effectiveness of focused intervention for priority groups

Beware of overdoing the 'we-are-setting-targets-and-measuring' approach when you have not yet set up a valid system to measure.

● Structure and systems
Questions

☐ Are the structure and systems appropriate? Check them out against the HMI's findings on pages 119–121.
☐ Do the working party meetings inspire people?
☐ Has all the work resulted in any change of practice?
☐ Are decisions being properly thought through?

Devise strategies to achieve and set targets for:

☐ Realistic deadlines within the school development plan for different stages of the policy to be achieved
☐ An effective staff training programme
☐ A properly-resourced policy
☐ Positive incentives for staff and pupils
☐ Embedding the policy in the school structure
☐ Monitoring lessons to evaluate progress.

● Creating a reading ethos
Questions

☐ Is literacy in the public eye? What is the image as you walk into the school and its classrooms?
☐ Do the walls reflect the ethnicity/gender/interests of the students in relation to literacy?
☐ What time does the school make for reading via tutor time, assemblies etc.?
☐ Is the library central to your approach? (Consider access etc.)
☐ Are parents involved?
☐ What literacy-related events are there?

Devise strategies to achieve and set targets for:

☐ Curriculum staff involvement
☐ Tutor involvement
☐ Reading/literacy-related events
☐ Quality of displays, with a view to keeping literacy in the public eye
☐ Development of library use/level of borrowing
☐ Involving parents
☐ Positive incentives for students
☐ Positive incentives for staff
☐ Student enthusiasm for reading/writing.

● Departmental practice and teaching methodology

Since literacy is the key to improving learning and raising standards, the central element of the whole-school approach must be to improve the quality of teaching throughout all curriculum areas. Targets and structures should be set up that focus on this aim.

Questions

☐ What training programme has been set up to spread good practice in literacy across the curriculum and help each area integrate literacy into its lesson planning and delivery?
☐ What opportunities are there for teachers to observe other teachers teaching?
☐ What opportunities are there for heads of departments to monitor progress?

Devise strategies to achieve and set targets for:

☐ Literacy targets within overall planning for each year (building up from Year 7)
☐ Literacy targets within unit planning year (building up from Year 7)
☐ Literacy supportive classrooms
☐ Encouraging reading related to subject.

● Overall student progress
Questions

☐ Do you want individual targets for all students or for specific groups of students?

Devise strategies to achieve and set targets for:

☐ Year-by-year targets for year groups building on baseline test information
☐ Raising student enthusiasm for reading and writing
☐ Involving students in the development of policy
☐ Awarding student progress.

● Effectiveness of focused intervention for priority groups
Questions

☐ Using baseline testing, what progress is being made by individuals in this group?
☐ Is progress maintained once students are no longer part of the focused support system?
☐ Is suitable support in place for EAL students who need help with English?

Devise strategies to achieve and set targets for:

☐ Monitoring the progress of individual, identified students
☐ Level of attendance of students on focused programme
☐ Maintaining targets once the programme has been completed
☐ Involving of parents of SEN students in scheme
☐ Mobilising of support from older students, parents, outside mentors, other staff.

What is a useful target?

All Targets should be SMART

Specific   – clearly defined and understood by appropriate audience (student, parent, staff, governors)
Measurable   – unambigusous, so that you know if the target has been hit
Achievable   – over-ambitious targets are discouraging; under-ambitious targets waste time
Relevant   – to the specific audience(s) for the target (student, parent, staff, governors)
Time limited – a target is not a target if there is no deadline

Within this general framework you need to consider whom the audience is for any target, and word the target appropriately for this audience.

The following was taken from an SEN student's individual education plan (IEP): *'Have access to a broad and balanced curriculum to achieve her level of ability'*. What is wrong with this as an IEP target?

If the key audience for the target is the student, it should be written with this in mind. I this case another significant audience is the parent. If the targets are for IEPs, a third relevant audience would be the class teacher, who is supposed to be able to use the targets to guide lesson planning to help the student progress.

Activity

Context: setting appropriate targets for Year 7 students on the literacy intervention programme.
Bearing in mind the points made above, work in pairs to grade the targets below. Use the following grading system:

Ex = excellent

OK= reasonable, but could be improved

X = useless

☐ Settle into mainstream secondary school and display appropriate behaviour.

☐ Seek teacher support when you don't understand something.

☐ Learn ten new spellings per week and attend Spelling Workshop to achieve a spelling age of 8.6 by the end of the year.

☐ Improve reading and spelling ages by the end of the year.

☐ Extend pieces of written work over the year to the appropriate level.

☐ Read daily to an adult/friend for ten minutes, putting expression into your reading.

☐ Learn ten new spellings per week and record them in a personal dictionary.

☐ Attempt all homework set.

☐ Improve homework completion to an acceptable level.

☐ Improve reading and spelling age to 8+ in the term.

☐ Develop literacy skills and apply them to the curriculum.

☐ Read on a regular basis at home.

☐ Improve quality of written presentation.

☐ Read to an adult for at least ten minutes per day.

☐ Do all work set sensibly and without fussing and cussing.

Running an effective introductory INSET day on literacy

The current attention to language and literacy practices focuses on methods of teaching. The development of a successful whole-school literacy policy should focus on making literacy an integral part of lesson planning and delivery across the curriculum. Changing practice takes time. Planning, providing training and allowing time for this change should be the foundation of any school approach to literacy.

One effective way forward is to use a training day as the initial springboard for planting ideas in each department. These can then be developed over time by a well-structured follow-up programme of staff development and decision-making such that all teachers understand how to make improving literacy underpin their lesson planning and delivery. Alternatively, the same input could be focused initially on a few departments and built outwards from there, or specific departments could use the materials provided to train their staff in how to integrate literacy into their unit planning.

Whether the 'involve-everyone-from-early-on' style is favoured or the 'develop-certain-areas' route is selected, you will need a series of practical ways to help get departments started. The materials that follow are easily adaptable for a range of approaches. From this point on, they will be presented as if the training day approach for all staff had been chosen. Wherever a page is marked as a handout it is assumed that the teachers and others involved in the training will be provided with this material. A possible outline for the first a day is provided (see Template 6, page 18). This will need to be adapted to reflect the specific circumstances of every school.

Literacy day invitation checklist

- All teachers (including headteacher)
- All classroom support staff
- Librarian
- Enthusiasts from the general support staff
- School governors especially the literacy governor
- Representatives from feeder primary schools
- Representatives from other local secondary schools
- Educational publishers

It is crucial to involve as wide a group of staff as possible in a literacy training day. Internally all the teachers, including the headteacher, should attend the whole day. Every teacher has plenty of work that they would like to get on with and many are resentful of training days for this reason. It is therefore important that the day is constructed to be as practical and positive as possible and that all school managers recognise its importance.

As well as all the teachers and the librarian, try to involve as many of the support staff as possible. Any classroom assistants should be there, but it may also be a good idea to see if any other support staff would be interested. At one school in Shropshire, the school caretaker led some of the school's National Year of Reading activities. If you have a literacy enthusiast on your support staff, involve them.

Invite the governors, especially the literacy governor (see Appendix 6, page 140). The more understanding the governors have of the issues, the more constructive a role they can play.

Invite representatives from feeder primary schools. This helps to build curriculum links and can be most constructive. Invite representatives from other secondary schools. This helps to broaden perspectives and encourages the sharing of good practice to the benefit of all.

It is also useful to invite educational publishers, since this enables staff to look at a range of curriculum materials in far more relaxing circumstances than the average rushed break on a teaching day. (This added to the effectiveness of the two-day literacy training programme at a school in Hull.)

Maintaining focus

It is a serious error to try to focus on more than one thing on a training day if teachers are expected to take concrete action as a result of the training. In the case of whole-school approaches to literacy, the long-term aim is to significantly affect how teachers plan and deliver their lessons. Such changes will only occur if sufficient time is given to them. Half-days of training on literacy, unless they are part of a well-structured ongoing programme of training, can give the wrong message to staff, telling them that the management has not yet understood the significance of what they are taking on.

Presenter's notes

Teachers really welcome training days spent as outlined on Template 6, page 18, and recognise the need to spend a full day considering good practice and developing effective teaching strategies. When planning your day's INSET, you clearly need to decide what elements you wish to include. Template 6, page 18, provides you with a programme outline plus some possible adaptations to consider. The programme on the left-hand side includes the three key elements of a whole-school approach:

- ☐ Creating a reading ethos
- ☐ Ensuring there is an effective intervention programme
- ☐ Involving all curriculum areas.

The main focus is on the last element. You may wish to miss out the first two strands from your whole-school training day and just focus the input on establishing literacy as a priority and what this means for all curriculum areas. The workshop element of the day is essential if teachers are to begin to adapt their planning and practice in the light of the morning's input. Remember that the processes you will be outlining need to be developed over time so that they become integrated into the planning and delivery of lessons across the curriculum.

Draft day's literacy training programme

Programme outline

Interactive session (1.5 hours)

1 <u>Priority</u>: establishing literacy as the key priority

2 <u>Ethos</u>: creating a reading ethos
- involving tutors in the process

3 <u>Support system</u>: recognising the need to set up effective support for students with literacy problems

4 <u>Curriculum areas</u>: making literacy a part of the curriculum
- Building on the literacy hour

Break: 30 minutes

(4 continued – 1.5 hours)

- Involving all curriculum areas: DARTs, writing frames, etc.
- Practical tasks for the afternoon and tasks to develop the initiative in each area

Lunch: 1 hour

Afternoon session

5 <u>Departmental workshops</u> (1.5 hours) Workshop session for each subject area in the main hall on developing existing units of work focusing on how best to develop the language (spoken, written and read) as appropriate.

6 <u>Plenary session</u> (30 minutes) – **Feedback from each area**

Possible adaptations

1 **Priority:** could be omitted, but the centrality of literacy would need to have been dealt with at an earlier time.

2 **Ethos:** could be omitted, but if so it needs to be dealt with at a separate time. It could form the basis of a training session in its own right, especially if the reading working party route is selected.

3 **Support system:** could be omitted, but would need to be the focus of discussion and training for the group running any intervention programme. All staff need to be aware of the nature of this and how their lesson planning could support the approach.

4 **Curriculum areas:** this section lies at the heart of any whole-school approach. All curriculum areas would need to consider the issues raised in this section. It could be broken into a number of parts, for example, by selecting those aspects that just focus on the spoken word and vocabulary.

5 **Departmental workshops:** it is essential to include a practical session within any such training programme to allow teachers to start applying the ideas that have been presented.

6 **Plenary:** it is advisable to conclude with a plenary session as it helps the working party plan the way forward, and can be inspiring.

The centrality of literacy to raising achievement

The centrality of literacy in education is summed up by an admiring critic's comment on the back cover of Alberto Manguel's *A History of Reading*: 'To read is to fly: it is to soar to a point of vantage...'. Just think about this image. If you can read well and use your literacy to develop and structure your thoughts, all the ideas of humanity over the centuries are available to you. You can select what you are interested in and challenge what you do not agree with. Think of the enjoyment that being able to read and respond has brought to your life and imagine a life where all the doors that literacy opens are closed.

Improved literacy is the key to making a real difference in children's lives. A student who struggles with reading and writing at secondary level will tend to struggle in all subjects. A literate student will achieve more effectively across the curriculum and is liable to have higher self esteem. The key issue is to reduce the number of young people leaving school who lack the basic competence to play an effective role in this highly-literate society. In short, teachers must ensure that our children leave school capable of soaring to a literate 'point of vantage'.

The vast majority of teachers recognise this centrality of literacy – that language is pivotal to learning. Many are held back not because they think it unimportant, but by a lack of confidence in how to improve things. Sometimes this manifests itself in blaming others for the 'problem', especially the English and Special Needs Departments. Again, the best way forward is not to debate the issue directly, but to present all staff with a practical way forward. Once they can see that it will be beneficial to the delivery of their part of the curriculum, the resulting boost in confidence will bridge the divisions and make a whole-school approach possible.

All teachers use spoken language to communicate their subjects and most also rely heavily on the printed word and writing in a variety of forms to convey their subject. Their students need to be helped to use the language of their subject appropriately. Improving literacy is the job of every teacher. Understanding this and acting on it will not make the job of teaching less demanding, but it will make it more satisfying.

Any staff grouping will have its own particular mix of the following:

☐ The enthusiasts who may already be well ahead of you
☐ The cynics who have 'been there, done that and know it doesn't work', so they are certainly not going to try again
☐ The hard-working but exhausted who are very willing to run with an idea if they can see that it will benefit the quality of their teaching
☐ Those who lack confidence in a range of teaching skills but would adapt if given the necessary help.

Getting as many of these groups as possible to appreciate the centrality of literacy to effective teaching has to be task number one. It will then automatically become a priority.

◢ Presenter's notes

One way of doing this is to show teachers the connection between effective teaching and literacy-related processes. Template 7, page 21 helps to achieve this. (This list is a summary of the findings of research from Sheffield University by Elaine Millard, Julia Davies and Ann Clark on the approaches found to be effective in improving boys' performance. It had the full heading 'Some ways of working in school to improve boys' performance'. For more information about boys' attainment, see Appendix 3, pages 123–125: *Boys and achievement*.)

☐ Using column A on Template 7, and covering up columns B and C, ask the teachers what they think the missing heading of the template would have been. Someone will probably say they think it is a list of the ingredients of good teaching. Discuss this.

☐ Then uncover column B of Template 7, which has the original heading 'What works with boys'. Staff should also be provided with Template 7, columns B and C, as a handout.

☐ Ask what the teachers would change if you were to compile a similar list for girls. (You will probably get a response, 'I wouldn't change anything.' Certainly this is the view shared by a wide range of teachers on this question.)
Now refer the teachers to the handout version and ask them in pairs to discuss whether all the processes listed are in any way literacy-related. They should indicate their decisions in column C using the key provided.

It is a useful checklist for teachers to bear in mind during the afternoon workshop session, when they will be adapting a unit of work. They will need to consider whether all the elements listed on Template 7 are part of their unit planning. When I have added another column headed 'Is it an integral part of the literacy hour?' the primary teachers who have completed the activity have said that all aspects of the list are integral to the hour. They do, however, recognise that making learning memorable can depend on far more than this and that access to ICT is an aspect of the hour that needs developing.

Establishing literacy as the key priority

If schools are to be effective, they need to have a clear view of their key priorities, rather than drowning in a sea of priorities and not making progress with any of them. If this is the case, funding will be spread too thinly and significant initiatives will lack the resources needed to make them successful.

◢ Presenter's notes

Using the Priority grid (see Template 8, page 22) can help establish why literacy should be a key priority for any school. The grid can be used either in pairs, in groups or introduced to the whole staff to show the necessity of having clear priorities to guide action. Use the grid as follows:

☐ List the possible school priorities in the same order on both sides of the grid (as per Template 8).
☐ Take the first issue on the left-hand side, **Literacy**, and discuss its relative priority when compared with the next issue which, in this example, is **Attendance**.
☐ Divide ten marks between the two to indicate which is the more important. (One person may argue that if

children do not come to school then there is no point in worrying about literacy and want to give 7 points to attendance and only 3 points to literacy. Someone else could retort that perhaps problems with literacy underlie many poor attenders' unwillingness to attend and therefore reverse the scoring, allocating 7 points to literacy.)

☐ Record your group's final decision on the grid. The first line records literacy's scores and so, if the final decision is to allocate 7 points to literacy and three to attendance, that should be recorded as shown in the example.

☐ Complete the grid, comparing each priority with the next in turn.

☐ Add up the final scores for each category and you have a clear priority order.

The whole purpose is to argue the issues in the hope of achieving a clarity and consensus that motivates staff to focus effectively on the school's key priorities.

Why literacy usually comes out as number one

Literacy is not an initiative on a par with others, but rather a key strand that should run through all the work of schools. It is the issue that underpins many other potential priorities, as can be seen from the discussion on attendance above. Raising achievement and boys' underachievement are two further areas which, when analysed, have a very significant literacy involvement. Indeed, this remains true wherever your school is within the league tables, since all schools wish to raise achievement and literacy is key to this.

The consequences of literacy being the key priority

The grid can only be introduced on a full training day since completing it is quite a lengthy process. The senior management team and individual departments may wish to take the time to complete the grid fully before or after the day. Once the school has established its key priorities, action is needed to trim down the priorities' list accordingly. If your key priority is literacy, then the money and time that has been allocated to other priorities may need to be redirected to support it. Literacy underpins so much that is central to school effectiveness that establishing a whole-school approach to literacy that really works will not be a one-off action, but rather the foundation of many other initiatives in the foreseeable future. If staff are not involved in thinking which issues really are priorities, then it is likely that they will just appear to be acquiescing to management's priority list, while quietly continuing with their own.

How to avoid a plethora of initiatives

The more you consider the issue, the more impossible it becomes to separate out literacy from improving the quality of teaching and learning, or from raising achievement. It therefore becomes sensible to combine these issues into the work of the literacy working party. Recent Government initiatives like 'Excellence in Cities' could then be embraced by the same working party, which may need to set up focus groups to follow particular strands.

What's the heading?

A What's the heading that describes these aims?

- Varying groups for different tasks
- Explaining the point of the lesson at the beginning
- Summing up what has been achieved at the end
- Clear instructions at each stage
- Small steps
- Short-term achievable goals
- Writing frames
- Support for homework
- Variety in each lesson and over the course
- Increased access to ICT and media work
- Relevance and variety of texts
- Clear guidelines to improve work
- Incorporating drama and oral work
- Making learning memorable

B What works with boys

- Varying groups for different tasks
- Explaining the point of the lesson at the beginning
- Summing up what has been achieved at the end
- Clear instructions at each stage
- Small steps
- Short-term achievable goals
- Writing frames
- Support for homework
- Variety in each lesson and over the course
- Increased access to ICT and media work
- Relevance and variety of texts
- Clear guidelines to improve work
- Incorporating drama and oral work
- Making learning memorable

C Is this a literacy-related process?

Activity

Working in pairs, use the following symbols to fill in the column below:

Y = definitely literacy related
Y? = literacy-related but...
X = not related to literacy
? = unsure

Priority grid

Grid to help select key priorities

	Literacy	Attendance	Punctuality	Student targets	Cross-curriculum themes	Raising achievement	Pace of lessons	Extracurricular offer	Boys' underachievement	TOTAL
Literacy		7								
Attendance	3									
Punctuality										
Student targets										
Cross-curriculum themes										
Raising achievement										
Pace of lessons										
Extracurricular offer										
Boys' underachievement										
TOTAL										

Raising the profile of reading

A central part of your literacy policy should be creating a reading ethos. This means raising the profile of reading and literacy for staff as well as students. The experience of some schools suggests that one person's determination to involve all staff and students in a reading initiative can turn a whole school round and transform it into a successful learning environment. Undoubtedly the key to this, as with any successful teaching, is enthusiasm. An enthusiast from the literacy working party could be given the time and resources to lead the implementation of some of the following:

Promoting literacy checklist

- Keeping literacy in the public eye.
- Making time for reading (involving all staff via tutor programme and assemblies).
- Giving the library a central role.
- Involving parents.
- Providing competitions, events and challenges.

Keeping literacy in the public eye

Some secondary schools can be quite depressing environments with very little on the walls to suggest that learning might be fun, interesting and challenging. The walls of most primary schools and many secondary schools tell a very different story. In the main foyer, displays give the message that reading and literacy are valued and this is iterated in every part of the school as each department illustrates its enthusiasm for its own subject area. The fact that books are available to be borrowed to increase interest in subjects should also be made obvious. Displaying large images of a variety of people reading a range of texts can help bring this message home.

Resources

This can be further reinforced by the effective use of role models exèmplified by the National Year of Reading's posters of football and TV stars promoting reading. (To order these free posters ring: 0845 6022260 – order no: NYRP2.)

Making time for reading

Tutor involvement will be supported and strengthened if a focus on reading is maintained through the school's assemblies. Some schools get a whole range of staff, students and parents to talk about texts that are important to them. (See pages 26–31 for training materials on involving tutors with reading.)

Giving the library a central role

The school library should be central to your policy. Maximising students' access to the library needs to be considered. The possibility of timetabling Year 7 lessons there, plus a rolling programme of lower-school registration, are two options that may aid this.

Libraries are excellent places for research, but staff need to reflect on whether students have been taught how to conduct research there effectively. Increasingly this will include how to search the Internet and how to select and download appropriate material. Where geographically possible, schools should also involve their local libraries to encourage students to use them regularly.

Involving parents

It is now well recognised that attitudes at home affect the development of children's literacy. The more encouragement a child has from home to engage in the reading process, the more likely they are to be literate. Parents want to help their children, but many lack the confidence to do so.

The best opportunity to invite parents to become partners in a secondary school's reading programme will probably be at the new intake interviews. This link can be strengthened by introducing reading cards that aid home–school communication. Including a column on the cards for children to express their views on their reading books is also useful, as in the following example:

Date	Title and Author	Pages	Score out of 10	Parent's signature

The reverse of the card includes the student's name, tutor group, related award scheme and a space for comments from parents. For more suggestions on involving parents see Template 9, page 24.

Providing competitions, events and challenges

Presenter's notes

Competitions and events are an excellent way of keeping literacy in the public eye and maintaining momentum. The school could consider putting on such events as those outlined in Template 9, page 24, or taking part in the annual national/international events referred to in Template 10, page 25.

The literacy working party will need to consider how all of these areas are to be developed – all of which have significant management implications. It may be worth giving one member of the working party the responsibility (and time) to carry out the work related to creating a reading ethos. The case studies on Template 10, page 25, give an outline of possible ways forward. Presenters may wish to reproduce these for the working party to consider. One approach is to ask the group to brainstorm the school's strengths and weaknesses on this issue. Use the 'Promoting literacy checklist' on this page to help you focus on the areas that the group needs to consider. Once you have established your areas of weakness on this issue, ask the group to work in pairs to highlight any of the various approaches to building a reading ethos, suggested on Templates 9 and 10 (pages 24 and 25 respectively), that they think would help rectify these weaknesses, plus any other suggestions they may have. Once you have established some possible ways forward, refine your list and decide what needs to be done to put it into action.

Creating a reading ethos

Keeping literacy in the public eye

Ensure the walls of the school celebrate reading. The foyer of Chaucer School, Sheffield, has images of the school students, teachers, cooks, cleaners, etc. all endorsing good reads.

Suggestions for involving parents

(Based on the schools feature of the NYR *Literacy Today Special*)

☐ Distribute copies of the DfEE's *A Little Reading Goes A Long Way – Helping with your child's reading* at Year 7 events to Year 7 parents and have them available at other parents' evenings.

☐ Make the reading and writing curriculum more visible and intelligible to parents through open days, classroom visits, videos, exhibitions and workshops.

☐ Recognise children's out-of-school reading by encouraging children to bring in examples of what they read at home.

☐ Increase children's reading opportunities at home by having more books available that can be taken home, or by running bookshops.

☐ Add to children's enjoyment of reading by encouraging parents to talk to their children about what they are reading.

☐ Encourage parents to be reading role models. Ask them to make a point of reading in front of children. Invite them into classes to talk about books they read as children or as adults.

☐ Bring a dad to school day to listen to children read/join reading events.

☐ Help parents who have reading difficulties themselves. Establish a climate in which parents can admit to difficulties without embarrassment. Be prepared with practical responses such as offering a 'Brush Up Your Reading' course in school or by acting as a bridge to local adult basic education provision.

☐ Schools wishing to establish or link up with family literacy programmes to help parents help their children will be able to find out about what programmes exist in their area on www.literacytrust.org.uk and search the literacy database. You can look at a summary of approaches to family literacy on: www.literacytrust. org.uk/Database/famlit or contact the Basic Skills Agency for information on its family literacy programmes (BSA, Commonwealth House, 1–19 New Oxford Street, London WC1A 1NU, tel. 0171 405 4017, fax. 0171 404 5038, tel. 0870600 2400).

Providing competitions, events and challenges

(Based on the schools feature of the NYR *Literacy Today Special*)

☐ **Set aside time for reading:** Park Hall School, Birmingham, set aside 40 minutes one day for everyone to read. 1,600 students, 101 teachers, the nurse, cooks, cleaners, caretakers and admininstration staff all took part. In the build-up to the event, students wrote to their favourite celebrities to discover which book they would choose to read, receiving hundreds of responses. Everyone in the school was talking about what they were reading and displays gave 'reading profiles' of adults who worked in the school, in whatever capacity. The success of the 'Time to Read' initiative was demonstrated by an increase in the number of books students read.

☐ **Invite an author to stimulate interest:** Milham Ford School, Oxford, is a comprehensive school for girls that used the visit of author Beverley Naidoo on World Book Day in April 1998 to do some cross-phase work with Marston Middle School. Students from Milham Ford were selected to participate in the workshops by submitting an entry for the school story-writing competition. Students from Marston spent the day at Milham Ford in the newly refurbished library. The morning involved studying Beverley Naidoo's famous novel *Journey to Jo'burg*, which all the students had read, and exploring plot and character analysis. A creative story-writing workshop followed, leading to some exciting stories. The students went away with their imaginations fired and a door to their creativity unlocked.

☐ **Organise story events with local libraries/bookshops** in which the whole school participates.

☐ **Hold lunch-time reading clubs** pairing older and younger reading partners.

☐ **Hold a book fair in partnership with other local schools:** ten schools in Minsthorpe, Pontefract, did so and were astounded by the enthusiasm of the children: 'It was as if they wanted to devour the books – as though they had been starved of their own books'. Follow this up by pairing up the schools so that students exchange book reviews and then display the work in local shops/libraries.

☐ **Arrange events for parents:** provide suggestions about how to encourage their child to read more, supported by displays of books, and competitions such as matching the teacher with his or her favourite poem or book.

☐ **Involve sporting heroes**

☐ **Involve businesses:** Post Office employees all over the country are released to work with young children. (A wide range of businesses is involved in supporting reading and mentoring in schools. Information on this is available from the National Literacy Trust's website: www.literacytrust.org.uk/Database).

☐ **Begin some staff meetings with a five-minute book slot** in which everyone recommends a recently read book to someone sitting nearby.

☐ **Explore *Boox*:** the magazine in which teenagers write reviews about the books that worked for them. The magazines producer, Well Worth Reading, recently ran a project that linked up the library service with the youth service to show how socially excluded youth can be turned on to reading. For details about *Boox* and the project's practical handbook with tips that will be useful to schools, contact Well Worth Reading, 15 Quarry Road, Winchester, Hampshire SO23 0JF; tel. 01962 865102).

Case Studies: Building a reading ethos

Wakeman School in Shropshire established a Reading Across the Curriculum Working Group to raise the profile of reading. The group shared a profound belief in the importance of reading. The headteacher chaired the group, which has representatives from most areas, but no area was press-ganged into membership; everyone participated because of their enthusiasm for the initiative.

Work organised by the group:
- Planning in-service training.
- Surveying boys' and girls' reading. The results were analysed and, as a result, library lessons became more focused through the introduction of reading diaries. There was a greater emphasis on non-fiction texts as a way of encouraging boys to get into the reading habit.
- Surveying the reading demands of each curriculum area. An example of the type of question posed was: 'To enjoy science at the highest level, what kind of reading skills are necessary to take this interest forward and sustain it?'
  Once the group had established what reading skills were needed, the next question was, 'Where is each skill taught?' This process established that some of the required skills were not being taught in any area.

The Wakeman School also etablished a National Year of Reading group to celebrate reading. Half the group consisted of teachers, the other half were support staff. Involving all staff gave a clear message about reading to the students – and some of the school's most avid readers turned out to be the support staff. One caretaker's enthusiasm for sport led to an excellent input from a local outdoor activity shop.

Other activities arranged by the group:
- Speakers on the literacy of their area
- Parents talking about reading
- Regular displays, including books chosen by students
- Assemblies where staff presented books that had been significant to them
- Reading days when every lesson started with a short extract from a book
- Every department identifying one unit of work per year in which they promote literacy or teach an aspect of reading; this could include research, note-taking, or wider reading
- Interviews with students about their attitudes to reading
- Regular reading time every day to make a public statement about the importance of reading (providing some boys with an excuse to be seen reading if they feel it lacks credibility).

St George Community School in Bristol set up a three-year Literacy Improvement Project. This started with Year 8 students, giving them a new subject called 'Achievement'. Teaching groups were small and set according to ability, with the least able groups working on phonics and spelling and the more able groups on more demanding comprehension, grammar and writing tasks. All of the groups read silently every week as part of the programme. The school also aimed to create a reading culture through the use of reading volunteers who hear children read for 10 minutes each week, with support from the 'Reading Is Fundamental' programme, which provided books for the students to take home and keep (see page 142). After the first year, test results showed a marked improvement in reading and spelling.

Hillside School, Hertfordshire has a pro-active approach to encouraging reluctant readers. Imaginative book displays around a theme, a returns trolley which gives the message 'other people like these books' and graphic novels stocked on the same trolley to attract the less keen boys, all encourage book borrowings.

Raising the profile of reading in a school could include taking part in key national/international reading events every year.
For the academic year 1999–2000 these are:
- **National Children's Book Week:** October 4th– 8th, 1999. This is co-ordinated by the Young Book Trust, which produces a pack of promotional materials and activities. YBT, Book House, 45 East Hill, London SW18 2QZ, tel. 0181 516 2977.
- **World Book Day – 23rd April** For more details fax 01634 290175 or look on the website: www.worldbookday.com.
- **Poetry Day:** The Poetry Society runs National Poetry Day, the Young National Poetry Competition and membership schemes for schools (tel. 0171 420 9890 – the Poetry Information Line, or contact the Poetry Information Society at www.poetrysoc.com).

Readathon, the sponsored national read, is now in its fourteenth year. It is often used by schools as part of National Children's Book Week. Children undertake to read books of their choice in return for pledges of money. It raises over £1 million annually to help sick children and is a proven way of stimulating children to read recreationally. Enrolled organisations receive a Readathon pack at the start of September (available from PO Box 89, Chipping Norton OX7 4PR, tel. 01608 730335).

For a whole range of resources to help build a reading ethos see Appendix 7, page 142.

The tutor's role in creating a reading ethos

Increasingly secondary schools are involving tutors in whole-school approaches to literacy and, in particular, reading. If the school is to give a consistent message about the importance of reading, involving tutors is essential. Since the tutor is seen as a form of 'home base' for students, and research shows that children are more likely to see reading as important if they come from homes where reading is valued, then there is all the more reason to involve tutors in the process.

Perhaps the greatest contribution that tutors can make is to encourage children to see reading as fun and to encourage conversations about reading To fulfil this role effectively, tutors will need access to good texts (i.e. texts that reflect the interests, choices and ethnicity of the group).

Schools taking part in the summer schools programme are expected to use tutors to oversee the literacy targets of pupils in the intervention programme. Training teachers both in the setting of these targets and monitoring will be necessary in many schools. For target setting, <u>Template 5 on page 16</u> can be used; see also the relevant presenter's notes on page 12.

Creating a supportive ethos

Any training should begin by helping the tutor to set up an environment where reading is non-threatening. Creating a positive atmosphere, where students are confident that any shortcoming in their reading skills will not lead them to being humiliated, is crucial to this. Remember that if you enter secondary school without being able to read at a reasonable level, you will probably feel negative about it and nervous of being humiliated. For this reason teachers should be careful when asking students to read aloud to the whole class (one headteacher in Swansea, who learnt to read very late, told me that his primary school existence had been dominated by his attempts never to be picked on to read aloud). Reading should never be used as a control mechanism. Moreover, if you choose to read around the class, be aware that many students will then not listen to the text, but will focus on the piece they may be called on to read. One way to establish a supportive ethos is to tell a story about when you have made a complete idiot of yourself when reading aloud. Normally this breaks the ice and begins a flood of stories from the group about being embarrassed by reading. This then presents an opportunity for the tutor to establish with the group that rule number one for any reading session must be 'Not in any way to mock someone because of mistakes they make in reading'.

Establishing group views about reading

To move everyone in their group forward, tutors have to know what they actually think about reading. If some students in the group hate it, the tutor will need to know this and why they feel that way.

Presenter's notes

Gary's account in <u>Template 11 on page 28</u> is a useful way of eliciting these views. Tutors could use this in the following way:

- ☐ Read Gary's account to the group, and then encourage a discussion about their early memories of reading.
- ☐ Get everyone to write their own version of the reading autobiography using the opening words 'I took to reading like…' and including some information on what their hobbies are. (If there are very poor writers in the group, then they can tell their story to a partner who can act as scribe for them.)

If well introduced, this piece of writing should tell the tutor who dislikes reading, and why, and give them a way in to start to interest everyone. Again, resources are crucial here because you will need books that reflect the interests of the students, especially those who do not feel interested in reading. So, if fishing interests them, then books or magazines about fishing will be a good way of helping them enjoy reading.

Silent reading and alternative strategies

Finding time for reading within the crowded school day is crucial, but enforced periods of silent reading can be problematic. Silent reading time can easily deteriorate into the teacher's sole role being that of silence enforcer. The teacher often sits at the front pretending to read while endlessly scanning the class for signs of deviation from silence. In such circumstances poorer readers sometimes just learn to be silent and turn pages in a 'look-look-I'm-reading' manner when glared at. A further complication is that if the teacher breaks the silence to talk quietly to a child about their reading or hear someone read, this is often taken as a general signal for talking. This could just reflect on my teaching skills, but I have seen enough teachers nod in recognition of this and heard enough children describe what it is they actually do when seemingly reading in silence to think there is a problem.

Activities

The following strategies present alternatives to silent reading in tutor groups:

- ☐ Paired reading
- ☐ Talking about reading
- ☐ Celebrating the languages of your group
- ☐ Making reading fun.

Paired reading

An effective alternative is to include paired or group reading within the reading sessions. Those who wish to read silently may, of course, do so. Others who find it easier to stay involved if they are reading in a pair or group can quietly do so. Group reading, i.e. groups reading in unison, can be a good way of supporting poorer readers since they are not being called on to read out loud alone.

Presenter's notes

Such group reading provides a supportive reading frame. Template 12, page 29, gives some useful hints to the class about how to be a supportive partner when being involved in paired reading.

Talking about reading

Reading in tutor time, which often equals registration time, can be complicated because time is short. A good use of this 10- or 15-minute slot is to get conversations going about good reads. (The Resources section of the National Literacy Trust's website – www.literacytrust.org.uk/resources – includes sections on specialist children's bookshops and useful organisations, as well as an EAL section that schools should find useful for purchasing dual language texts and texts in English reflecting the ethnicity of their students.)

Most readers' reading habits are greatly influenced by the books that friends recommend to them. Book groups where students talk about what they have read can be an excellent way of encouraging more reading. Each group could decide on its 10 best reads and then discuss their selections with other groups. Older students could visit younger groups to recommend the books they had liked when they were that age. The walls of the tutor group could reflect the group's reading choices. Do not restrict students' choices to fiction. Some boys have resorted to reading information books under the table because of a belief that this was not considered proper reading.

Resources

An excellent resource here for older students is Well Worth Reading's magazine for teenagers, *Boox* which is full of book reviews written by teenagers. Its irreverent tone, powerful design and celebrity input makes a huge impact on teenagers. They say they like the way *Boox* relates reading to contemporary culture and they devour the book recommendations (Well Worth Reading, tel. 01962 865102; fax 01962 853747).

Celebrating the languages spoken in each tutor group

Developing the languages that pupils speak is central to their developing literacy. Tutors should be aware of all the languages that students in their group can speak and whether they can read and write in them. Some teachers feel ill at ease about this and, as a result, tend to gloss over the issues. This can add to some students' tendency not to reveal the languages that they can speak because they feel they do not have credibility. Such a lack of self esteem about an issue that is so fundamental to a students' sense of self is very damaging. Tutors need to help overcome this problem.

Activities

Use Template 13, page 30 to introduce a simple activity that all tutors can use to celebrate the range of languages within their tutor group. The template consists of *The cat sat on the mat* written in English and then a range of other languages. Explain that you create your tutor group's version of this list in the following manner:

- ☐ Write on the board the simple sentence: *The cat sat on the mat*
- ☐ Underline the subject, *cat*
- ☐ Put a circle round the verb, *sat*
- ☐ Put a wavy line underneath *mat*

- ☐ Ask pupils to come up and write the sentence in as many languages as the class represents, marking up the sentences appropriately. (They may need to ask a member of the family to write it for them if they speak, but cannot write, the language. In addition, of course, a few languages do not have a written form.)
- ☐ Use an arrow to indicate the direction in which the text should be read if it differs from English.

You will then start to build up a list like that on Template 13, page 30 which shows English, Turkish, French, Welsh, Urdu, Gujerati and Cantonese.

Once you have established your list, transfer it to a poster for your tutor group room. It can then be updated if you get a new member of the group who speaks another language. This helps to give status to students' other languages (one tutor group cheered when a boy arrived who could add a new language to the class's list). Having such a list is more appropriate than those posters saying welcome in a multiplicity of languages, because this poster is personal and accurately reflects the ethnicity and language knowledge of the group.

The list can lead to an interesting discussion about the structure of language. This visual representation of the structural differences between languages offers a good opportunity to get the class thinking about the structure of languages. It starts people asking questions like: 'How do they know which is the cat in the second language?' (Turkish). It may be that you won't be able to answer some of these questions, but that's part of the point: the questions get students thinking about the fact that the structure of language relates to its meaning.

Making reading fun

Most of all, tutors can encourage the idea of reading as fun. The best way of doing this is not by *saying* that reading is fun, but by *making* it so. Tutors may need help in gaining the confidence to do this. A great way to start is by reading a play.

One play that is ideal for this is *Flat Stanley* (Penguin Education). Stanley becomes 'flat' as a result of the bookshelves above his bed collapsing on him. Looked at from the front he is normal but from the side he is only a few centimetres in depth. The play is a series of chapters relating the adventures of this flat boy. The parts are all relatively easy to read, with the role of Arthur being the easiest. As with much good children's literature, the text is very witty.

Presenter's notes

Ask members of staff to read the extract from *Flat Stanley* on Template 14, page 31 and ask them how they would get a child who was a very reluctant reader to take part in this play-reading successfully. One obvious solution is to coach your Arthurs so that when it is their chapter they can read their role effectively and come in with the right timing and intonation. This could be that child's first experience of public success at reading aloud. Such things are crucial in the building of confidence.

I took to reading like a duck takes to water.

I've always found it an enjoyable experience and, as I've grown older, I've read more and more.

The first books I read were *Peter and Jane*. I found these incredibly boring compared with the books my mum would read when I went to bed. My mum read me *Mr Men* books and Enid Blyton stories. My favourite stories were set in a magic faraway tree. It was a land where chocolates grew on trees and the rain came down as 'pop' which I found incredibly amusing.

I would fall asleep dreaming myself into the story and often finding my dreams more adventurous than the stories themselves. This gave me encouragement to express myself in the last year of infant school and on into junior school in the way of writing stories.

The *Mr Men* stories were also highly sought after bedtime reading. I would struggle through reading the books with my mother egging me onwards. After reading a *Mr Men* book at night time, to have to read a *Peter and Jane* book the next day seemed a completely worthless experience. I would speed through these books with the greatest of ease but because, in my haste to get through the reading matter in front of me, I would make the occasional error, my teacher mistook this for lack of ability and would say:

'Now, Gary, that isn't how it goes, is it?

I know,' I would try to tell her.

But she would carry on: 'Now say it slowly.'

'Yeaaaaaaaas, Miss. "Peter kicked the ball at the window".'

'Well done! See, you can do it if you try.'

I couldn't believe my teacher could be so naive, no, even stupid, in believing I couldn't read 'window'. But still my infuriating teacher insisted on my reading yet another tedious *Peter and Jane* book.

Gary W (aged 14)

How to help your partner improve their reading

How to encourage your partner

- Try to listen as carefully and encouragingly as possible.

- If you have read the book yourself, introduce it. Comment on its title, its theme and aspects that interested you.

- Encourage your partner to use all the clues in the book like pictures and context.

- Do not interrupt your partner when they alter a word if it has nearly the same meaning as the word written down, for example, reading house for home.

- Notice if your partner is having difficulty with more than one word out of every 10. If they are, suggest that they choose a slightly easier book.

- Encourage your partner to read in phrases and sentences thus bringing out the meaning of the words. This will help the reader and listener understand the text.

- Give your partner a few seconds before helping them with a word. Then. rather than saying the whole word for them, try to break it down into parts or syllables. This will help them to get it right for themselves. For example, with unhelpfully, cover up the beginning and end of the word so that first they see help then helpful then helpfully. By then, they should be able to recognise the whole word for themselves.

How to put your partner off

- Yawn and mock your partner if they make a mistake.

- Make your partner read a book they are not interested in.

- Make them sound out every word.

- Find as many mistakes as possible in their reading to emphasise what a genius you are and how hopeless they are.

- Make them keep reading the book even though they clearly cannot.

- Let your partner read word for word ignoring the punctuation and without making any sense of the text.

- Instantly tell them every word they pause over.

English

The cat (sat) on the mat.

Turkish

Kedi kilimin üstünde (oturdu.)

French

Le chat (s'est assis) sur le tapis.

Welsh

(Eisteddodd) y garth ar y mat.

Urdu

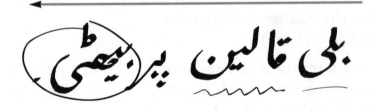

Gujerati

Cantonese

Flat Stanley

Mrs Lambchop:	Stay on the pavement, boys. Owwwww! I've dropped my ring. It's rolling across the pavement towards that grating. * Quick! Get it!
Stanley:	Arthur! Arthur! Get it quickly.
Arthur:	I can't. It's gone.
Mrs Lambchop:	Oh Stanley! Oh Arthur! It's my favourite ring and now it's dropped between the bars of the grating. It must be down at the bottom of the shaft.
Stanley:	Don't cry! I have an idea. Look! I've got some laces in my pocket. I'll tie them together. Now I'll take the laces out of my shoes and make one very long string.
Mrs Lambchop:	What are you going to do, Stanley?
Stanley:	I'm going to tie one end of the long lace I've made to the back of my belt. You hold the other end. Now, slide me down.
Mrs Lambchop:	Do you mean I've got to lower you down between the bars?
Stanley:	Yes, that's it. I'm so flat, you can slide me down between the bars so that I can look for the ring.*
Policeman:	Hullo, hullo! What's going on here? What's the matter lady? Is your yo-yo stuck?
Mrs Lambchop:	I'm not holding a yo-yo. I'm holding my son, Stanley.
Policeman:	I've never seen a lady holding a shoe lace over a grating before. This son of yours must be a very funny shape.
Mrs Lambchop:	Shame on you. My son is searching for my ring. Not every mother has a flat son to send looking for lost rings.
Policeman:	I'd better be careful what I say to this poor soul. Are you sure you feel all right, lady?
Mrs Lambchop:	Of course I'm all right. It's my son who's not all right. He's down there in the dark.
Policeman:	The poor soul's as dotty as can be!
Stanley:	Hooray! I've got it! Pull me up!*
Arthur:	Good for you, Stanley.
Stanley:	Whoops! Here I am! And here's the ring.
Policeman:	I didn't get it lady. I'm sorry.
Mrs Lambchop:	I know you didn't get it. My son's the one who went down and got it.
Policeman:	I mean, I didn't understand.
Mrs Lambchop:	Dotty, indeed! You called me dotty. Shame!
Policeman:	I was too hasty. I see that now, and I can see that you have a very flat son.
Mrs Lambchop:	People should think twice before they make rude remarks, and then not make them at all.
Policeman:	That's a very good rule, lady. I'll make a note of that and remember it.

* = sound effect required here

(from Flat Stanley adapted by Sheila Lane and Martin Kemp from the story by Jeff Brown)

Effective support systems for students with literacy problems

Raising all teachers' awareness of literacy, and how to plan lessons so as to best develop the language and literacy related to each subject area, is at the heart of improving teaching and learning in all subjects. It should therefore particularly enhance the educational experience of students who need to catch up with their basic literacy skills, as well as all other students. In the words of Neil Smith, Special Needs Inspector at the Camden Key Stage 3 Literacy Conference, *'This is the most exciting opportunity for developing special needs across the curriculum in the last twenty years.'*

On its own, quality teaching of literacy across the curriculum will not enable students who have fallen significantly behind in reading and writing to catch up. Hence the importance of an effective early-intervention programme to help these students become independent learners as part of a whole-school approach to literacy. The national focus on literacy must not be allowed to widen the gap between the literacy haves and have nots. The 20–30% at the tail end of achievement must not be allowed to drift ever further behind. Setting up an effective intervention programme is a subject that requires a handbook to itself. Given the focus of this book, therefore, there is only space to concentrate on a few key points before returning to the central theme of enabling all teachers to consider the literacy aspects of their subject.

Of all the disputed areas within the secondary curriculum, whether to temporarily withdraw or fully integrate pupils with literacy difficulties has probably caused the greatest controversy.

Practice has veered between extremes. Thirty years ago withdrawal was the order of the day. This then became reviled and inclusiveness became the watchword for much of the 1980s and 1990s, enhanced by intonation of the phrase 'access to the curriculum'. This approach has much to recommend it, but it can also mask the fact that some students may not be able to access the curriculum because of their literacy problems. These children are in danger of becoming alienated from the education process without a focused intervention to help them become independent learners. By the mid-1990s, a mixed approach was becoming generally more accepted.

Recent research has shown what the experience of many teachers bears out: children who have failed to crack the basics of reading and writing by the end of their primary education will not suddenly catch up in the secondary classroom, even if there is a programme of in-class support. They will need an intensive focused programme of withdrawal to help them reach a level of reading and writing ability that will enable them to cope independently in the classroom.

In England there is now a requirement for all schools with Key Stage 3 students to have an intervention programme for students transferring from primary school who have failed to reach the level expected for their age (Level 4).

'It is vital that work in the early stages of Year 7 recognises pupils' prior attainment. Pupils who are likely to struggle in meeting the literacy demands of the Key Stage 3 curriculum need urgent attention to improve their reading and writing skills.'

(from the school file manual supporting the NLS Key Stage 3 Literacy Conferences)

In many schools in England, intervention will be linked to the summer literacy programme that has been extended to cover 900 schools. Schools not taking part in the programme will be expected to have an intervention programme with a similar focus to that outlined on page 33. Trying to rectify the 'long tail of underachievement' has relevance throughout the UK.

Creating an effective intervention programme for students is an important area for consideration by the literacy working party. Focused programmes of support for students with reading and writing difficulties have considerable resource and planning implications. The Key Stage 3 manual referred to above contains much useful information about setting up effective intervention programmes. This will be added to as the further evaluation of the Key Stage 3 projects becomes available. A summary of the intervention programme linked to the summer schools follows.

Resources

A useful pamphlet on support for students with literacy problems is *What Works in Secondary Schools – Catching up with Basic Skills*, published by the Basic Skills Agency (tel. 0171 404 4017). This includes a range of recommendations supported by illustrations of how they have been put into practice.

Useful information on the effectiveness of intervention schemes is offered in *What Works for Slow Readers: The effectiveness of early intervention*, by Greg Brooks, Nicola Flanagan, Zenta Henkhuzens and Dougal Hutchison (NFER). This research focuses on students who have fallen behind in the early years of the primary sector. The findings therefore refer to primary-age students but their relevance to the secondary sector is clear. The following conclusions were reached; the first is, perhaps, the most important.

☐ Normal schooling ('no treatment') does not enable slow readers to catch up.

☐ Work on phonological skills should be embedded within a broad approach.

☐ Children's comprehension skills can be improved if directly targeted.

☐ Working on children's self-esteem and reading in parallel has definite potential.

☐ IT approaches work only if they are precisely targeted.

☐ Large-scale schemes, like BSA family literacy and Reading Recovery, though expensive, can give good value for money.

☐ Where reading partners are available and can be given appropriate training, partnership approaches can be very effective.

Further information on the findings of research is available on the National Literacy Trust's website: www.literacytrust.co.uk/Database/whatworks.

First Steps initially developed effective intervention programmes in Australia for the primary sector. It now offers training on intervention programmes for the secondary sector.

Intervention programmes from summer literacy schools

Background to the literacy schools

Summer literacy schools were first funded by the Government in England in 1997 when 50 schools took part in a pilot scheme involving at least 50 hours of tuition for students. The following year the numbers were increased ten-fold with over 500 schools taking part. In 1999 the Government went ahead with a £13 million programme involving 900 schools and 27,000 students.

The two key differences between the 1999 summer literacy schools and those of previous years were that they had to be:

- Closely linked to the methodology and content of the literacy hour
- Followed up by an intervention programme at Key Stage 3.

The Secretary of State for Education, David Blunkett promised new, 'sharply focused' teaching, emphasising phonics, spelling and grammar. The evaluation of the earlier schemes had shown that they significantly boosted the confidence of the students involved, but failed to raise the reading levels of 45% of participating students.

Taking part in the programme

The following information is taken from the 'Guidance for Providers of Summer Schools' (see Appendix 7, page 141) to give schools that did not take part in the scheme an outline of the key elements of the programme. This is suitable for consideration by the working party or relevant subgroup when working on how best to ensure the school has an effective intervention programme for students who need support with literacy.

The focus of the programme was students likely to transfer to secondary schools with levels of attainment in English below Level 4. Funding for this programme was allocated by the LEA to secondary schools. Participating schools were required to set up a school literacy management group in order to:

- Co-ordinate contact with partner primary schools and the parents of children involved
- Support the administration of the summer literacy school
- Audit existing literacy provision in Year 7
- Carry out action-planning and target-setting, orchestrate whole-school provision including allocation of resources
- Organise staff training
- Monitor and evaluate the overall programme
- Ensure that literacy work had high status in the school and was viewed positively.

The 1999 summer schools were built around:

- At least 50 hours of dedicated literacy teaching
- Work planned against key objectives drawn from the NLS Framework for teaching
- Teaching closely based on the organisation and teaching strategies of the literacy hour
- Target setting, assessment and rewards that motivate students to succeed.

Planning for the Year 7 curriculum: this was intended to provide bridging activities to boost students' reading and writing skills and minimise the risk of regression at transfer. Suggestions for such activities:

- Holiday study packs for students unable to attend the summer literacy schools
- Literacy-based projects linking work in the summer term in Year 6 with work in the early autumn of Year 7
- A reception programme including meetings with parents; contact with tutors who would be monitoring and supporting students' progress in literacy across the curriculum; informing students about personal targets and reward systems; and literacy diaries to help students plan and monitor their own progress.

The Key Stage 3 intervention programme

This included:

- Planning to key objectives drawn from the NLS Framework for teaching
- Tightly structured lessons based on the NLS model
- Withdrawal in small groups of particular students for additional literacy lessons linked to the main teaching programme
- Additional support tailored to meet students' needs: for example, reading support programmes involving volunteers; spelling and handwriting clubs; short intensive programmes
- Guidance for subject teachers on how to support students' literacy development across the curriculum
- Periodic review meetings with students to monitor progress against agreed targets.

The monitoring and evaluating process included:

- Diagnostic assessment of reading, writing and spelling drawing on information from Year 6
- Individual target setting and review
- Periodic cross-curricular review of progress in literacy with reporting to students and parents
- Testing at the end of Year 7.

Resources

A more detailed outline of this approach is available from the DfEE, entitled *Guidance for Providers of Summer Literacy Schools and Key Stage 3 Intervention Programmes for Literacy 1999–2000*.

Presenter's notes

Template 15, page 35, is from the school file manual supporting the NLS Key Stage 3 Literacy Conferences. It encourages schools to consider the elements of any intervention programme and the practical implications of each of the strategies in supporting students working below Level 3, at Level 3 and above Level 4.

If your school is not taking part in this year's summer literacy programme and related intervention programme, it would be useful for the working party or appropriate sub-group to consider how many of the elements listed on Template 15, page 35, are already in place in the school. This list covers the required elements of the formal intervention programme, and could be worked on in two ways. Those elements that are in place could be highlighted in one colour, and analysed to see which target group they serve, their effectiveness and any outstanding practical implications. The group could then focus on those that are not in place and discuss their relative importance. These could then be listed in order of importance and the group could focus on deciding how they are to be implemented. The practical implication column is obviously of particular importance here. Withdrawal programmes for specific groups have significant timetabling implications.

The following summary of the key points to bear in mind when planning your intervention programme should prove useful. The working party may wish to use this as a checklist to establish how the school plans to meet these points. It is developed from the ideas of Elizabeth Plackett, Education lecturer, Goldsmith's College.

Planning intervention programme strategies checklist

- Ensure effective screening and diagnostic procedures and use information from primary schools.

- Organise effective focused support for those who struggle with literacy.

- Recognise that focused support will require priority status when planning and timetabling the curriculum.

- Establish clear targets for students with literacy difficulties.

- Inform teachers of these targets so they can plan and mark work accordingly.

- Avoid narrow approaches to teaching literacy.

- Provide good quality books for inexperienced readers.

- Involve parents.

- Mobilise as much support as possible – older pupils, parents, outside mentors, staff.

Key elements in intervention planning

Intervention strategy	Target group			Benefits	Practical implications
	2–	3	4+		
Close contact with partner primary schools to identify students likely to need support					
Profile of students' strengths and weaknesses in literacy					
Bridging projects					
Literacy summer schools					
Summer literacy packs					
Designated literacy lessons, using the *Framework* and planned to specific literacy objectives					
Withdrawal programmes, providing a short intensive programme of guided reading and writing					
Explicit attention to literacy in other subjects					
Literacy targets and review					
Extra-curricular support, using volunteers to provide homework clubs, literacy clinics, paired reading opportunities, etc.					

Involving all curriculum areas

The materials detailed below should all be covered on a training day aimed at launching a whole-school approach to literacy, showing as they do how all teachers can play their part in implementing this. The ideas put forward should then be developed over time so that they become integrated into the planning and delivery of lessons across the curriculum. The materials provided in this book are presented as follows (page numbers are shown on the right):

Improving transfer to the secondary sector

Presenter's notes

All teachers will need to build on what the children have learnt in primary school. This is particularly important in England because of the changes that the literacy hour has made to the content and delivery of literacy.

Templates 16 and 17 (pages 37–38) have been provided as handouts to give teachers a brief explanation of the hour. They are meant to be taken away and read by teachers. In presenting them on a training day, focus on the processes of the hour that are summed up by the clock. Stress that the literacy hour has revolutionised the way that many primary teachers in England teach. This is because of the clear teaching framework for literacy, and the structure of the hour that accentuates making learning objectives explicit and encourages:
- Direct teaching
- Teacher modelling
- Pace
- Student reflection on learning.

Referring to the clock diagram (Template 17, page 38), talk teachers through what that hour actually means. The section of the video referred to in 'Resources' on this page is particularly useful here for helping teachers to understand the direct teaching mode of the opening thirty minutes of the hour.

One of the aims of extending the National Literacy Strategy to the secondary sector was to rectify the loss of momentum for students when they transfer from the primary to the secondary sectors. This has long been identified by researchers as a significant problem. Its key causes have been identified as:
- Insufficient awareness by secondary teachers of students' needs and competences
- The change of culture and organisation between the school sectors
- Lack of curricular continuity
- Differences in teaching styles.

Any whole-school approach to literacy and related intervention programme will need to bear these points in mind when planning a curricular approach for the new intake.

Resources

Secondary schools throughout England have been sent copies both of the literacy hour framework (in a folder) and the accompanying training materials (in a white plastic box). Both are available from the DfEE, see Appendix 7, page 141. The density of this information, plus the pressure of work on teachers, means that understandably much of this excellent information may have remained in the box in many schools. Ideally, the school's literacy co-ordinator will be able to select key aspects of the box to present to secondary colleagues.

Particularly useful to staff are the opening three sections on Video 2, since these deal with the importance of grammar and show two talented teachers teaching the literacy hour. This will help teachers understand the processes underlying the hour and how focused the teaching of skills is.

Presenter's notes

Template 18, page 39, is the outline from the framework showing the syllabus to be covered in the last term prior to the students' transferral to secondary schools. This provides a very useful summary of the scope of the literacy hour and the level of understanding of the structure of English that is expected from the students. All secondary teachers will need to be aware of this and, in particular, all teachers will need to build on the students' understanding of the structure, language conventions, and the grammatical features of the different types of text as they are outlined here. This is dealt with in more detail later in the book (see pages 40–44).

The significance of the literacy hour and National Literacy Strategy

The literacy hour has revolutionised the way that many primary teachers in England teach. This is because of its clear teaching framework for literacy, combined with the structure of the hour, that accentuates making learning objectives explicit, direct teaching, teacher modelling, pace and time for student reflection on learning. This will increasingly mean that students transfer to secondary schools with a far greater understanding of a wide variety of text. Students are being encouraged to read as writers, thus they will also be able to write at a more sophisticated level in a range of non-fiction, as well as fiction, genres and possess the technical terminology to express this understanding. They will rightly expect their secondary teachers to build on this knowledge across the curriculum. Having become accustomed to pacy lessons with excellent group control, so that they move quickly between activities, they will expect this standard to be maintained and developed in their new school. All secondary school teachers in England therefore need to have a general understanding of the literacy hour, with English and SEN teachers needing a more specific understanding. The following is also useful background information for secondary teachers from other parts of the UK.

The development of a literacy strategy

☐ 1996: The National Literacy Project was established in England by the Conservative Government through the Department for Education and Employment. It was piloted in a number of schools in selected LEAs in England. Led by Director John Stannard, its purpose was to raise standards of literacy in line with national expectations for primary schools by improving the quality of teaching through more focused literacy instruction and effective classroom management. Work in the classroom was to be supported by improving the school management of literacy, including target-setting linked to systematic planning, monitoring and evaluation.

☐ In the lead-up to the 1997 general election, the Labour Party identified education as a very significant issue. It set up a working party led by Professor Michael Barber to look in particular at literacy. This group produced a document prior to the election called *The Reading Revolution*. It highlighted a range of initiatives aimed at raising reading standards, including Reading Recovery, and suggested the need for a National Year of Reading. However, its key emphasis was on the significance of the National Literacy Project in the battle to raise standards.

☐ *The Reading Revolution* went out to consultation and was finally published as the National Literacy Strategy in September 1997. The literacy hour is the lynchpin of England's National Literacy Strategy which, in the first instance, focused on the primary sector. From September 1998 all primary schools in England were expected to implement the literacy hour though it is not a legal requirement to do so.

The thinking behind the literacy hour

The National Literacy Project was based on research and inspection evidence since 1986 that had identified key factors in improvements to standards of literacy at primary level.

At school management level, better literacy standards were associated with:
☐ High expectations based on aims and targets and evaluating the school's progress
☐ Detailed, practical schemes of work, with clear planning procedures
☐ The effective use of time for literacy work
☐ Systematic monitoring of teachers' work by senior staff
☐ Practical training and support for teachers
☐ Effective use of additional adults
☐ Close involvement and support of governors.

At classroom level, better literacy standards were associated with:
☐ A clear focus on instruction through direct teaching
☐ Careful classroom management to maximise the direct teaching time and reduce the amount of time teachers spent controlling and reacting to students
☐ Systematic and challenging teaching of phonics, spelling and vocabulary at both key stages
☐ Systematic teaching of a range of extended reading skills and non-fiction reading at Key Stage 2
☐ A close connection between teaching and reading
☐ Coverage of the full range of reading and writing required by the National Curriculum.

Common patterns and routines

The literacy hour is based on a highly-structured, detailed scheme of term-by-term objectives (called the framework). This covers the range of required work, common procedures for planning and the use of time, and training and support through a national network. The strategy is designed to support individual teachers, but is also expected to bring about institutional changes. Thus each school is required to have a detailed strategy for implementing the work, including staff training, support, the use of additional adults, the timetabling of literacy lessons and monitoring and evaluating progress towards the school's declared targets.

The framework of the literacy hour

The structure of the hour

The basic structure of the hour is the same for all classes so that students meet a predictable framework and experience similar routines as they move classes or schools (see literacy clock below). It provides teachers with a common structure to share for planning and the development of ideas. It also enables teachers to be more proactive in the classroom and maximise the time spent teaching, as opposed to managing. The structure encourages pace in lessons. The framework provides a clear focus for teaching, with each lesson beginning with a specific objective.

The processes encouraged by the hour

A central feature of the hour is the use of big books or the over-head projector, which facilitate a whole-class reading of one text. Such an approach enables the teacher to model reading and thinking processes for the students. This modelling is strengthened at the end of each lesson when students review what they have learnt. During this plenary session students internalise the processes that they have been involved in, just as a driving instructor's repetition of the step-by-step instructions helps the learner remember the stages involved in the driving process.

Evaluation

National Curriculum tests have shown that 50% of the pilot schools improved faster than the national average and about 30% did significantly better. In some schools the hour has had a domino effect, improving teaching throughout the school.

Teachers' response

Reaction to the literacy hour throughout the country has been increasingly positive with teachers recognising the benefit of having a structured framework to guide them and gaining confidence about their ability to help students read and write. Generally students have responded well to the structure and expectations of the hour.

It should be remembered that schools had limited time to digest the training material. Some teachers felt it would have been better to have had a year to familiarise themselves with the training materials before implementing the programme in full. In addition, they felt that there could have been more flexibility in allowing them to use their professional judgement to adapt the hour to the needs of their students. Others were concerned about the narrowing of the curriculum and felt that literacy should not be boxed into the literacy hour, but needs to be spread throughout the primary curriculum.

Undoubtedly, as teachers become more familiar with the literacy hour, their professional judgement will become crucial in adapting the hour so that it can accommodate both extended reading and writing, especially creative writing.
Overall, many primary teachers now feel that they are in a better position to intervene effectively in improving the literacy standards of the students.

Moreover, the focus and pace of the hour, combined with an increased understanding of literacy and how this underpins all learning, has influenced the approach to teaching right across the primary curriculum. If possible, the literacy co-ordinator of every secondary school should see the literacy hour in action in primary schools, as well as showing video clips to all teachers.

The structure of the literacy hour

The focus of lessons is divided between
- ☐ Word level work:
  Phonics, spelling and vocabulary
- ☐ Sentence level work:
  Grammar and punctuation
- ☐ Text level work:
  Comprehension and composition

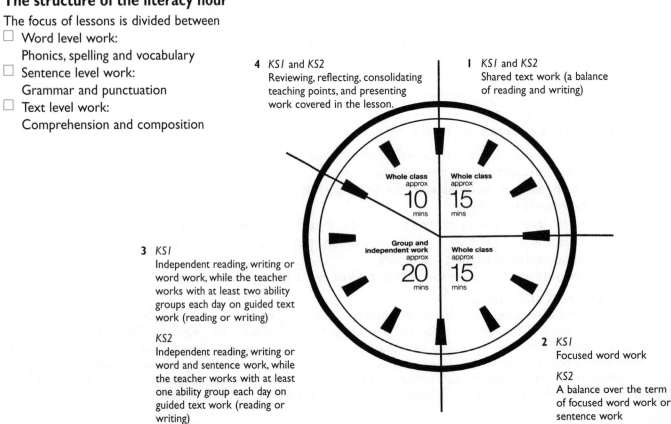

4 *KS1* and *KS2*
Reviewing, reflecting, consolidating teaching points, and presenting work covered in the lesson.

1 *KS1* and *KS2*
Shared text work (a balance of reading and writing)

Whole class approx **10** mins

Whole class approx **15** mins

Group and independent work approx **20** mins

Whole class approx **15** mins

3 *KS1*
Independent reading, writing or word work, while the teacher works with at least two ability groups each day on guided text work (reading or writing)

KS2
Independent reading, writing or word and sentence work, while the teacher works with at least one ability group each day on guided text work (reading or writing)

2 *KS1*
Focused word work

KS2
A balance over the term of focused word work or sentence work

National Literacy Strategy framework for term prior to transfer

Year 6
Term 3

Range

Fiction and poetry: *comparison of work by significant children's author(s) and poets: (a) work by same author (b) different authors' treatment of same theme(s).*

Non-Fiction: *(i) explanations linked to work from other subjects; (ii) non-chronological reports linked to work from other subjects; (iii) reference texts, range of dictionaries, thesauruses, including IT sources.*

Word level work: Phonics, spelling and vocabulary
Pupils should be taught :

Spelling strategies
1 to identify mis-spelt words in own writing; to keep individual lists (e.g. spelling logs); to learn to spell them;
2 to use known spellings as a basis for spelling other words with similar patterns or related meanings;
3 to use independent spelling strategies, including:
   - building up spellings by syllabic parts, using known prefixes, suffixes and common letter strings;
   - applying knowledge of spelling rules and exceptions;
   - building words from other known words, and from awareness of the meaning or derivations of words;
   - using dictionaries and IT spell-checks;
   - using visual skills, e.g. recognising common letter strings and checking critical features (i.e. does it look right, shape, length, etc.);

Spelling conventions and rules
4 to revise and consolidate work from previous five terms with particular emphasis on:
   - learning and inventing spelling rules;
   - inventing and using mnemonics for irregular or difficult spellings;
   - unstressed vowel spellings in polysyllabic words;

Vocabulary extension
5 to invent words using known roots, prefixes and suffixes, e.g. *vacca + phobe = someone who has a fear of cows*;
6 to practise and extend vocabulary, e.g. through inventing word games such as puns, riddles, crosswords;
7 to experiment with language, e.g. creating new words, similes and metaphors.

Sentence level work: Grammar and punctuation
Pupils should be taught:

Grammatical awareness
1 to revise the language conventions and grammatical features of the different types of text such as:
   - narrative (e.g. stories and novels);
   - recounts (e.g. anecdotes, accounts of observations, experiences);
   - instructional texts (e.g. instructions and directions);
   - reports (e.g. factual writing, description);
   - explanatory texts (how and why);
   - persuasive texts (e.g. opinions, promotional literature);
   - discursive texts (e.g. balanced arguments);
2 to conduct detailed language investigations through interviews, research and reading, e.g. of proverbs, language change over time, dialect, study of headlines;

Sentence construction and punctuation
3 to revise formal styles of writing:
   - the impersonal voice;
   - the use of the passive;
   - management of complex sentences;
4 to secure control of complex sentences, understanding how clauses can be manipulated to achieve other effects.

Text level work: Comprehension and composition
Pupils should be taught:

Fiction and Poetry
Reading comprehension
1 to describe and evaluate the style of an individual writer;
2 to discuss how linked poems relate to one another by themes, format and repetition, e.g. cycle of poems about the seasons;
3 to describe and evaluate the style of an individual poet;
4 to comment critically on the overall impact of a poem, showing how language and themes have been developed;
5 to compare and contrast the work of a single writer;
6 to look at connections and contrasts in the work of different writers;

Writing composition
7 to annotate passages in detail in response to specific questions;
8 to use a reading journal effectively to raise and refine personal responses to a text and prepare for discussion;
9 to write summaries of books or parts of books, deciding on priorities relevant to purpose;
10 to write a brief synopsis of a text, e.g. for back cover blurb;
11 to write a brief helpful review tailored for real audiences;
12 to compare texts in writing, drawing out:
   - their different styles and preoccupations;
   - their strengths and weaknesses;
   - their different values and appeal to a reader;
13 to write a sequence of poems linked by theme or form, e.g. a haiku calendar;
14 to write an extended story, worked on over time on a theme identified in reading;

Non-Fiction
Reading comprehension
15 to secure understanding of the features of explanatory texts from Year 5, term 2;
16 to identify the key features of impersonal formal language, e.g. the present tense, the passive voice and discuss when and why they are used;
17 to appraise a text quickly and effectively; to retrieve information from it; to find information quickly and evaluate its value;
18 to secure the skills of skimming, scanning and efficient reading so that research is fast and effective;
19 to review a range of non-fiction text types and their characteristics, discussing when a writer might choose to write in a given style and form;

Writing composition
20 to secure control of impersonal writing, particularly the sustained use of the present tense and the passive voice;
21 to divide whole texts into paragraphs, paying attention to the sequence of paragraphs and to the links between one paragraph and the next, e.g. through the choice of appropriate connectives;
22 to select the appropriate style and form to suit a specific purpose and audience, drawing on knowledge of different non-fiction text types.

Grammar training needs

All secondary school teachers need to be aware of the key literacy terminology and concepts that will increasingly be familiar territory for students transferring to secondary schools. (Coming your way soon may well be students with an understanding of the passive.)

This will require some in-service training in many secondary schools. Although teachers' implicit knowledge of the language will be very high, they may lack the explicit knowledge and therefore the confidence that will help them communicate grammar effectively to their students.

Many teachers under the age of 40 have not been taught grammar, while older teachers often have grim memories of being taught a highly theoretical form of grammar suited to Latin rather than English. The grammar that underlies the National Literacy Strategy's approach is functional grammar, full of practical everyday applications.

Many secondary schools until recently had ceased teaching the grammar of English. This led to many modern language departments feeling increasingly beleaguered. They have had to teach grammar from scratch before being able to turn to the specific grammar of the particular language they are trying to teach. Recently, these factors have convinced many of the need for in-service training in this area.

Presenter's notes

Template 19, page 42 lists most of the technical terms used in the literacy hour, and an explanation of how to use this list is suggested in the presenter's notes below.

Resources

The *Sentence Level Work* materials from the *NLS Literacy Training Pack* offers a very good starting point for providing teachers with a basic explicit knowledge of grammar. *The Grammar Papers*, offering some very interesting insights into how approaches to grammar have changed in the last 30 years, is available from the QCA.

Another useful publication is *Breakthrough to Learning: Linguistics in the service of Mainstream Education*, by Mary Mason and Bob Mason (Trentham Books). This practical book explains how linguistic theory can help develop language across the curriculum and presents the theory behind the Wigan Language Project.

A key question: 'Why teach grammar?'

In the words of Professor David Crystal:

'Grammar is what gives sense to language ... Sentences make words yield up their meaning. Sentences actively create sense in language. And the business of the study of sentences is grammar.'

(from Video 2 accompanying the *NLS Literacy Training Pack*)

Everyone who speaks English has significant implicit knowledge of the structure of the English language. But, without explicit knowledge, helping children to move forward so that they can write and speak in standard English, when appropriate, and read effectively can become very difficult.

We do not shy away from using technical terms in technology and maths, but for some strange reason we seem to have shied away from explicitly teaching the fundamentals of the structure of the language and its related vocabulary.

Consider this problem. A child has written: 'The flowers is blue' in a context that requires standard English. If the child is not familiar with the basic terms underlying the structure of the language, the parts of speech, then you are forced into statements that go something like this. Teacher: 'You've got to make that word agree with that word because there are lots of flowers so, it is "flowers are" not "flowers is". Try to remember this'. There is clearly no logic that a child can follow in a woolly statement like this, but doubtless they would smile pleasantly and give a good impersonation of understanding. The next time they write they would be left trying to decide what sounds best, which could be tricky territory, given the wide variety of colloquial English spoken throughout the UK. Children are aware of the range of registers within the language, but they need help to develop this awareness further. As has been long established, language is power and we do our children a great disservice if we do not teach them to feel confident in their use and understanding of their language.

Resources

Schools that have access to the *NLS Literacy Training Pack* may wish to watch and discuss the beginning of Video 2 with its interesting comments from the public on grammar, plus the short but illuminating statement by Professor David Crystal who is interviewed on the video. The Sentence level work from the same pack is also a very useful source of staff training.

Moving forward with grammar

Presenter's notes

1. Distribute copies of the literacy hour technical vocabulary list (Template 19, page 42) to all teachers and ask them to highlight any terms that they would not want to stand up in public and explain. (There is a big difference between thinking you understand a concept and being able to explain that concept effectively to students.)

☐ Unfortunately, the original list included some terms that are extremely obscure, such as, 'tanka', (apparently a slightly longer form of haiku). Such words somewhat undermine the fact that there is a functional reason for children becoming familiar with the majority of the technical terms on the list, i.e. helping them feel more confident about their understanding of language and providing them with the terminology to discuss it.

☐ Most of the literary terms have been removed from the list, since it is not these that teachers across the curriculum need to be familiar with. However, there will still be a whole range of terms that many teachers will not be familiar with, especially those relating to phonics. Making the glossary from the literacy hour framework document available to staff may be an idea, but definitions alone will not make them confident users of the concepts.

☐ Students have taken to the technical language of the hour with such enthusiasm that teachers have had to do the same by default. This has empowered the students and built confidence. They have the language to talk about things in a way they have not been able to before.

☐ This handbook contains a section on developing a whole-school approach to grammar (see pages 100–101) that you may want to consider at this point.

2 Using the extract from the Sentence Level Work pack in the *NLS Literacy Training Pack*, Template 20, page 43:
   ☐ Ask staff to read and discuss the passages in pairs
   ☐ Ask one pair what passage X is and then discuss their response
   ☐ Ask another pair what passage Y is and discuss their response.

☐ Identifying the first passage as narrative is easy – explaining how you know it is slightly more difficult. People normally point to the range of descriptive language used (adjectives and adverbs plus the use of direct speech). A useful observation that one Section 11 teacher made here is that 'You already know the tune'.

Learning the tune of each subject

Helping children know the tune of their subject (i.e. the structures that make up its typical language patterns) is the key thing that teachers need to achieve. Children are most familiar with the language of everyday speech that focuses on the first person (I/we), and may often use the present tense even when past events are being referred to, e.g. 'Anyway, I says to him, we're going to go whatever he says'. In contrast, the language of curriculum areas is usually much more formal and often consists of the third person (he, she, it), the past tense and is impersonal, e.g. 'Panama became a base in which to build ships to explore and exploit this unknown sea. It was the threshold of a vast expansion.'

Lessons should be structured to help children become familiar with these more academic language patterns. This is the main focus of the rest of this book. Every subject area needs to help students know the tune that represents the structure of language of their subject.

Singing from the same hymn sheet

It will help if all curriculum areas are using common terminology. It would seem sensible that secondary school English departments should strengthen the understanding of the function and structure of language that has been begun by the literacy hour in primary schools. This would leave the Modern Languages/Welsh departments to focus on the specific grammar that is necessary to understand the structure of other languages. For example, English does not have a dative (a syllable added on to nouns or pronouns to indicate movement towards, which replaces prepositions like 'to' in English). However, an understanding of the dative is necessary for comprehending a range of languages such as German, Turkish and, of course, Latin. Pages 100–101 include a section on building on the literacy hour's approach to grammar.

Resources
A useful resource here is *The Cheshire Cat's Guide to English Grammar* (available from Cheshire Teachers' Resources Centre (tel. 01829 741118). This contains a poster, like the one on Template 21, page 44, which can be put up in classrooms ostensibly to help the students, but also as a useful *aide-mémoir* for teachers.

Technical vocabulary from the literacy hour

The main technical terms used in the Framework for teaching are listed below according to the year in which they should first be introduced. Most of these terms should form part of the students' developing vocabulary for talking about language (the literary terms have been removed).

Word level

Reception: alphabet; alphabetical order; grapheme; letter; onset; phoneme; rime; sounds; word

Year 1: consonant; letter sound: final, initial; lower case; plural; spelling pattern; upper case; vowel

Year 2: antonym; compound word; digraph; prefix; syllable; synonym

Year 3: apostrophe; definition; homonym; root word; singular; suffix

Year 4: diminutive; font; homophone; pun; simile

Year 5: acronym; cliché; idiom; metaphor; slang; technical vocabulary

Year 6: mnemonic; proverb; word derivation

Sentence level

Reception: capital letter

Year 1: full stop; question; question mark; sentence; speech marks

Year 2: bold print; comma; exclamation mark; italics; punctuation

Year 3: adjective; bullet points; conjunction; formal language; grammar; informal language; noun: collective, common, proper; pronoun: personal, possessive; verb; tense; 1st, 2nd, 3rd person

Year 4: adjectives: comparative, superlative; adverb; clause; colon; connective; hyphen; paragraph; phrase; possessive apostrophe; semicolon

Year 5: dialect; imperative verb; preposition; rhetorical question; speech: direct, reported; standard English; subject

Year 6: asterisk, complex sentence; hypothesis, impersonal language; parentheses: brackets, commas, dashes; voice: active, passive

Text level

Reception: beginning; book; cover; end; line; page; recount; rhyme; story; title

Year 1: author; blurb; caption; character; contents; diagram; dictionary; fiction; illustrator; index; instruction; label; layout; lists; non-chronological writing; non-fiction; play; poem; predict; report; setting; signs

Year 2: anthology; explanation; fact; flow chart; glossary; heading; key phrase; key word; nonsense poem; notes; poet; publisher; riddle; scan; setting; skim; story; plot; verse; subheading; theme; tongue twister; alliteration; audience; bibliography; dialogue

Year 3: encyclopaedia; fable; legend; myth; parables; purpose of writing; sequel; sequence; structure; thesaurus; traditional story

Year 4: abbreviate; argument; chorus; debate; discursive writing; discussion; editorial; epitaph; fantasy adventure; free verse; jingle; monologue; narrative; opinion; persuasive writing; playscript; science fiction; summary; voice

Year 5: ballad; chronological sequence; complication; edit; extract; imagery; novel; point of view; quotation; resolution; rhyme; plan

Year 6: anecdote; appendix; autobiography; biography; commentary; footnote; journalistic writing; narrator; obituary; parody; personification; riddle; synopsis; viewpoint

(adapted from the NLS Framework for teaching)

Moving from implicit to explicit knowledge of language

The following extracts are adapted from the opening page of the training programme for primary teachers on *Sentence Level Work* pack from the *NLS Literacy Training Pack* produced by the DfEE as part of the National Literacy Strategy.

Session 1 – What is Grammar?

Fundered Dorblids

 Read texts X and Y below. Think about the different types of text (recount, report, explanation, instruction, exposition, narrative, poetry etc.). Discuss in pairs/groups what type of text each one is and what evidence there is to support your decision.

X Stanzic squored at the fundered Dorblid. It skilvered for a misken, then sliged into the wistap. Jista hazed durgily and sputtered, 'Stanzic, look at those granzic booblies.'

Y Fundered Dorblids make a full and distable parble that can be nured in pry tides.

icindels:

2 Dorblids
half a sedge
2 strills of crand

i) stump up the sedge with a blidling sling to set feckle;
ii) rout the Dorblids into foilds...

(adapted from the Sentence Level Work pack from the Literacy Training Pack, produced by the DfEE as part of the National Literacy Strategy.)

The Cheshire Cat's Guide to English Grammar
② Word CATegories

Grammar helps you to make words do what you want them to do. The job a word does in a sentence tells you its grammatical category, e.g. noun, verb, adjective, adverb. Some people call these categories parts of speech; others call them word classes.

Happiness is cat-shaped.
The **cat** on the **mat**.
I like **fish**, **cream** and **sleep**.
My **mother** is called **Tiddles**.
Cheshire County Council is based in **Chester**.

Nouns

Names of persons, places or things. Names of persons (Tiddles) and places (Chester) are proper nouns. All other nouns are common nouns. Things can either be concrete (fish, mat) or abstract (happiness).

Personal
I, me, you, she, he, we, us, they, them, myself, herself, himself, yourself, ourselves, yourselves, themselves

Impersonal
it, itself, they, them

Demonstrative
this, that, these, those

Pronouns

Words that can be used instead of nouns.

Grammatical Words

A wide range of words that join up all the others and keep them in order.

Articles
a, an, the

Prepositions
e.g. for, in, from, at, over, under

Conjunctions
e.g. and, but, then, because, if, when, although

Adjectives

Words that describe nouns. They can be simple (fat), comparative (fatter) or superlative (fattest).

I like **tinned** food.
Fish is very **good** for cats.
My love is like a **red**, **red** rose.
A **huge**, **black** cat.
A **little**, **old** lady.

Adverbs

Words that tell you how, when and where a verb is performed.

Adverbs also intensify adjectives (make them stronger).

She walked **quickly**.
He moves **quietly**.

Fish is **very** good for cats.
Mice are **extremely** tasty.

Verbs

Doing words – they tell you what is happening. But the two most common verbs are not 'doing words' in the obvious sense – they are 'to be' and 'to have'.

to be
am, is, are, was, will be, being, been, were
These are often used to help other verbs i.e. as auxiliaries

to have
have, has, had, has had, had had, having, having had
These are often used to help other verbs i.e. as auxiliaries

Cat **eats** dog. **Take** care.
I **came**, I **saw**,
I **conquered**.
Give me a good reason.
Keep smiling. I **like** ice cream.
She **means** it.

He **had walked** 10 miles.
She **will be chasing** mice,

Dictionaries tell you how to spell words and what they mean. They also give you grammatical information. Look out for the code, e.g. n = noun, v = verb, adj = adjective

REMEMBER
that a word can be used in different ways.
e.g. I think I'll cycle (*verb*) to school.
My cycle (*noun*)
is in the cycle (*adjective*) shed,
but it needs cleaning.

Teaching the literacy of each curriculum area

The following materials are aimed at helping students to improve their ability to access texts within each subject area. They are based on developing students' knowledge of context and the structure of language; in other words, the 'tune' of the language that goes with each curriculum area.

The complexity of the reading process

 Presenter's notes

Before moving on to look at how each curriculum area can contribute to raising literacy standards, it is first useful to consider the nature of the reading process. Template 22, page 48; has been designed to do this and could be presented as the following activity.

Activity

1 Ask different members of staff to read out loud passages 1 to 3 on Template 22, page 48. Then ask why they think it is so relatively easy to read these passages on sight, given that all three are very far removed from the received spelling of standard English. The answers you will receive will probably include the following:
   - ☐ Motivation
   - ☐ Prior knowledge
   - ☐ Context (the fact that all the passages have the same context means that the brain brings forward the appropriate vocabulary and related concepts for this subject, making them progressively easier to read).

Again in the words of that teacher come to mind: 'You already know the tune'.

This activity makes it clear that although phonics is important to the early stages of reading, becoming an established reader involves far more than phonics.

It is also worth remembering, when looking at passage 2, the relationship between typed text and the ability to read text easily. The combination of poor handwriting and poor spelling can make many students' work very hard to read. Access to word processors greatly eases this problem and boosts the students' confidence so that they are motivated to improve the spelling as well as the content of what they write.

2 Give staff a few minutes to read passage 4 on Template 22, page 48. Ask them if it is decodable in a reasonable amount of time. Then reveal that the text reads:
   'I typed this sentence to see how much the brain relies on the gaps between the words to help it decode text.'
   - ☐ It is worth telling the group this or some will spend the next fifteen minutes quietly conferring, trying to work it out. Of course the text also conveys the point about the importance of word spaces concisely.

3 Ask another member of staff to read out passage 5 on Template 22, page 48.

   In an entertaining way, this passage will reinforce the group's understanding of the complexity of the reading process, this time concentrating on how readers scan ahead, reading text in chunks, to gain the overall sense.

Resources

Passage 5 is taken from *The Languages Book* (English and Media Centre). This is a superb collection of material on language resulting from collaboration between the Institute of Education and the English and Media Centre. It is full of inspiring material that could provided excellent text for literacy lessons.

The introduction to the National Literacy Strategy Framework for teaching, by John Stannard, NLS Director, is well worth reading. Stannard explains (page 3) that:
'All teachers know that pupils become successful readers by learning to use a range of strategies to get at the meaning of a text. The principle is at the heart of the National Curriculum for English and has formed the basis of successful literacy teaching for many years. The range of strategies can be depicted as a series of searchlights, each of which sheds light on the text. Successful readers use as many of these strategies as possible.'

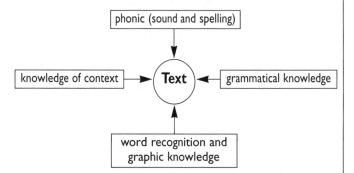

Delivering the literacy of individual curriculum areas

Each curriculum area should be encouraged to consider how to teach the literacy of its area, drawing on the good practice of other areas to increase the quality of the delivery of their own subject. Staff need to consider the specific literacy demands of their area and devise strategies to help make these explicit in lesson planning and delivery. Once this has been established, each subject area should set specific literacy targets for every year related to the literacy demands of each subject.

Resources

A useful planning resource is *Use of Language: A Common Approach* (available from QCA publications line 0171 509 5555) which was distributed to all secondary schools in England by QCA. Those schools that have used it recommend it highly. It consists of an overall school document plus accompanying leaflets for key curriculum area (except, interestingly, for modem languages whose omission it explains). The introduction stresses that:
'Work in each subject develops specific aspects of pupils' English, since all subjects include demands for specialist concepts and vocabulary and particular uses of spoken

*and written English. Each subject also develops pupils'
general ability to communicate as work is discussed,
speculations made, events described, processes reported
and explanations given. Helping pupils to say what they
want to say clearly, using vocabulary and grammar
accurately to do so, enhances and enriches teaching and
learning in all subjects.'*

(Use of Language: A Common Approach, QCA)

The following extract from the whole-school document
shows the sort of overview it provides:

A whole school approach should include:

☐ *developing a shared understanding between all staff of
the role of language in pupils' learning and how work
in different subjects can contribute to and benefit from
the development of pupils' ability to communicate
effectively*

☐ *helping teachers to be clear about the ways in which
their work with pupils contributes to the development
of pupils' communication skills*

☐ *knowledge and understanding of the pupils' standards
of achievement in speaking and listening, writing and
reading, and the identification of any areas of strength
and weakness*

☐ *taking account of the needs of all pupils, including the
more able, those with special educational needs and
pupils for whom English is an additional language*

☐ *structuring lessons appropriately in ways that support
and stimulate language development and showing how
learning objectives for pupils are to be achieved*

☐ *recognising how resources will be organised and used
to support this teaching*

☐ *monitoring and evaluating the impact of common
goals and clear, shared expectations of pupils'
developing ability to talk, read and write effectively
and, specifically, establishing whether targets have been
achieved.*

An example of the questions posed in the departmental
leaflets is provided below:

Design and Technology and the use of language:

☐ *In what ways can work in information technology help
to develop speaking, listening, writing and reading
skills?*

☐ *How can pupils' understanding of design and
technology be enhanced by developing these skills?*

(Both extracts from Use of Language: A Common Approach, QCA)

These leaflets were developed by practising teachers from
each appropriate area. They are full of practical suggestions
for improving teachers' awareness of the development of
language for their area.

Presenter's notes

Template 23, page 49 is taken from the introduction
and gives useful examples of the language features of a range
of texts. Presenters may wish to introduce this as part of a
training day. It could be used to help staff who are unclear
about the different sorts of text and their associated features.
Ask a non-scientist to read the top hand-written text. They
will probably stumble over the word alveoli because, given
the handwriting, it is not legible if you are not already
familiar with the word. This is a useful reminder of how

much handwriting can get in the way of our ability to read
words. Use the points made in the typewritten text above
this passage to draw attention to the structure of the text and
the importance of connectives.

Ask staff to read the middle passage to themselves. Draw
attention to the difference that choice of person makes when
writing. Good examples of this are provided in the
explanation above the text.

Ask another member of staff to read the bottom hand-
written passage. Use this and the typewritten text above it to
explain what the passive is and what effect it has on text.
Remember that a significant number of staff will not know
what the passive is. Explain that this page will help staff
consider the sort of language that is conventionally used to
express the subject that they teach.

Making staff aware of how unchallenging some 'work' can be

School audits reveal a worrying level of unchallenging
activities related to text, for example: meaningless copying
and poorly-constructed comprehension and cloze exercises.

Presenter's notes

One of the best ways to make staff aware of these
pitfalls is to look again at the typical findings of school
audits (see Template 24, page 50), this time not just stressing
the problems but also emphasising the final point: 'Good
practice that is not shared'. Then, rather than tell them
about comprehension and cloze exercises that are
structured so as to be meaningless or research that is merely
copying, let them experience these things in the following
activities.

Activities

1 Pointless comprehensions

This activity should be conducted in role-play mode
with both reader and presenter playing the role of an
insensitive bossy teacher.

☐ Ask a member of staff, whom you know in advance is willing
to do a performance reading, to read the text Corandic
(Template 25, page 51) in the worst sort of teacher voice –
one that suggests that anyone who doesn't understand is an
idiot.

☐ Following this rendition, ask your 'class' the five questions
underneath in a suitably peremptory tone encouraging the
chanting of replies.

☐ Ask them to write up Corandic for homework.

☐ Then discuss what this tells you about the nature of many
comprehension exercises.

☐ Stress that comprehensions can be useful: it depends on the
purpose of the exercise and how the questions relate to this
purpose. With this in mind, ask staff to suggest ways of
improving learning outcomes when preparing
comprehension questions.

2 Even more pointless cloze exercises

Warn staff to beware of 'overhelpful' cloze passages.
They can render the whole point of this type of activity
meaningless.

☐ Ask staff to fill in the blanks in The Peek-a-Boo World
(Template 26, page 52).

They will find that they can get full marks without understanding a word (unless they happen to be able to read Turkish). This may seem rather irrelevant until you consider that what the teachers atre required to do when filling in the "Peek-a-Boo World' is exactly what students are required to do by a best-selling science workbook for lower-ability Key Stage 3 pupils. The whole of the book consists of cloze passages that can be filled in correctly without ever having to read the text or have any understanding whatsoever of the processes described. It will be popular with many children because it will make them feel secure and popular with some teachers since it keeps children occupied.

Template 27, page 53 is an example of a constructive cloze passage where the gaps have been related to a defined purpose. In this case the purpose is a linguistic one – to practice using appropriate connectives. The first sentence of a well-constructed cloze should not have any gaps in it to help the reader get a sense of context.

3 And pointless copying

School audits of literacy reveal much meaningless copying of information. Use Template 28, page 54 to illustrate this. This was written by a girl with reading and writing difficulties who had chosen to do research on dolphins.

☐ Ask staff to identify what the problem is.

The complexity of reading strategies

Passage 1

Whxn wxll thx bxxks xrgxmxnt xnd? Sxrxly xt mxst bx clxxr thxt chldrxn usx x vxrxxty xf strxtxgxxs tx rxxd prxnt xnd thxt xn xndxrstxnding xf thx rxlxtxxnshxp bxtwxxn lxttxrs xnd sxxnds xs xnly xnx xf mxny strxtxgxxs.

Passage 2

It muts be fairyl obvoius to aynone raeding this that raedres draw on thier konowledge of how lagnuaeg wroks, thier abitily to recgonise wrods on sihgt and thier capcaity to ues contextaul cleus to enabel them to maek senes of what has goen befoer and perdict wath is cmoing next.

Passage 3

If y— can r— th— sure— you mu— agr— tha- a mix— appro— is nec———.

(adapted from materials by Kay Hiatt, English Inspector, Surrey)

Passage 4

(Note: There are no spelling mistakes in the following, but clearly x = a vowel or an x!)

xtypxdthxssxntxncxtxsxxhxwmxcht hxbrx xnrxlxxsxnthxgxpsbxtwxxnthxwxrd stxhxl pxtdxcxdxtxxt.

Passage 5

One of the mysteries about reading is how people can read so fast. That's because the brain doesn't look at every letter, work out what it means, and go on to the next letter. It reads print in 'chunks', skipping along the line, picking up things here and there, lightning fast. Your brain thinks ahead, working out what is liable to be ahead before it gets there. That's why proof reading is so difficult because you're accustomed to reading things that are full of mistakes without really noticing them: e.g.:

Reading is like a high-spede geussing game in which the readers brain tries to maek sence out of the funny black mraks on the paeg. It's the brian that dose the wrok not the boook. So even all if words the the on page get midex pu te bniar can ususayll wrok out what shud be ther. Clever tihng, the brian.

(from *The Languages Book*, The English & Media Centre, see Appendix 7, page 141)

Examples of language features from a range of subject-specific texts

- Simple sentences are effective in expressing single ideas or views that are straightforward, but as soon as greater complexity of thought is needed then particular grammatical structures will need to be used, e.g. 'then...', 'because...', 'however...', 'therefore...'. In such ways, sequential and causal relationships, contrasts or conclusions can be expressed. Such expressions represent key concepts in a number of subjects and students need to learn to appreciate their significance and use in context.

Science

> Nicotine and tar from smoking can severely damage your lungs. The nicotine affects the sides of the lungs, and therefore it also affects the alvedi. The lungs can then no longer control gaseous exchanges properly and breathing problems occurs— lung cancer etc. The nicotine also damages the hairs in the trachea which keep germs and dust out of the lungs. Because these hairs no longer work, tar builds up in your lungs, you then develop smokers cough.

- As students' writing develops, there will be increasing differences between speech forms and how writing is organised. Students do not always find impersonal writing easy; for example they may use 'you' ('*you need to mix the two chemicals together*') or 'I' ('*I watched the temperature rise*'), when the convention is usually to use impersonal forms that emphasise concepts and ideas.

D&T

> Friction can be useful or unhelpful. It is useful in a bike because the brake blocks rub against the tyres and create friction. It's unhelpful because a door on a carpet creates friction and makes it hard to open the door. Friction can be changed. For example, putting oil in a bearing makes less friction, and the bearing works better.

- Students are often unfamiliar with the passive form, so they are more likely to remark that 'they have organised the museum so you see the dinosaurs first' than 'the displays have been organised so the dinosaurs are seen first'. The passive suggests greater objectivity and detachment, which are particularly significant in technical and scientific subjects.

D&T

> In the 1970's the micro chip was invented. This opened a whole new era for businesses. and for storing information. It was said that three computers could do as much work as ten typewriters. The digital watch was also introduced and that soon put the swiss watch makers out of business

Many of the texts students read provide models of the styles and grammar that are appropriate for particular subjects, and students can draw on this experience in their own writing. Explicit teaching in this area reinforces learning and helps students to judge how best to organise their written work.

Typical findings of school literacy audits

Are they applicable to your school?

- **Lots of copying.**

- **Much unchallenging comprehension work.**

- **Students encounter a minimal range of texts.**

- **Reading is often restricted to short bursts of a few seconds.**

- **Writing usually consists of very short unfinished pieces.**

- **Students aren't taught how to use reference materials.**

- **Widespread use of worksheets – often ill-designed.**

- **Insufficient opportunities for oral work.**

- **Good practice that is not shared.**

Corandic

Corandic is an emurient grof with many fribs. It granks from corite, an olg which cargs like lange. Corite grinkles several other tanances, which garkers excarp by glarking the corite and starping it in tranker-clarped strobs. The tarances starp a chark which is expargated with worters, branking a slorp. This slorp is garped through several other corusces, finally frasting a pragety, blickant crankle: coranda. Coranda is a cargurt, grinkling corandic and borigen. The corandic is nacerated from the borigen by means of locacity. Thus garkers finally thrap a glick, bracht, glupous grapant, corandic, which granks with many starps.

Questions

1 What is corandic?

2 What does corandic grank from?

3 How do garkers excarp the tarances from the corite?

4 What does the slorp finally frast?

5 What is coranda?

(from Weaver, 1980)

 Activity

1 What does doing this tell you about the nature of many comprehension exercises?

2 Suggest some ways of improving the potential learning outcomes when preparing comprehension exercises.

Peek-a-Boo World

The peek-a-boo world

Fill in the gaps in the following text using the words from the box below:

"CE-EE" DÜNYASI

1800'lerin Amerikalıları mekân "fethetme" sorunuyla çok f_____ ilgiliydiler. On dokuzuncu y_____ ortasında sınırları Pasifik Okyanusu'na kadar genişlemiş, ilk adımları 1830'larda atılan gelişmemiş demiryolu sistemi insanlarla birlikte bütün kıtayı katetmeye başlamıştı. Gene de 1840'lara kadar enformasyon akışı ancak insanların beraberlerinde g_____ hızlılıktaydı; tam bir anlatımla, bir trenin götürebileceği kadar hızlı, daha somut bir ifadeyle, saatte yaklaşık otuz beş mildi. Bu s_____ nedeniyle ulusal bir topluluk olarak Amerika'nın gelişmesi bir ölçüde gecikti. 1840'larda Amerika hâlâ her biri kendi ağzıyla konuşan ve kendi çıkarlarının peşinde koşturan bölgelerden oluşuyordu. Kıta çapında bir konuşma modeli henüz mümkün değildi.

On dokuzuncu yüzyılın ortasına d_____ iki fikir biraraya geldi ve birbirleriyle yakınlaşarak yirminci yüzyıl Amerikası'na yeni bir kamusal söylem metaforu sağladılar. Onların birleşmesi Yorumlama Çağı'nın temelini yıkmış ve Gösteri Çağı'nın temelini atmıştı. Bu fikirlerden biri t_____. yeniyken, diğeri Altamira'nın m_____ resimleri kadar e_____ Eski fikri birazdan ele alacağız. Yeni fikir ise, ulaşımın ve iletişimin birbirinden a_____, enformasyon akışında mekânın kaçınılmaz bir kısıtlayıcı etken o_____. düşüncesiydi.

ayrılabileceği	**fazla**	olmadığı	yüzyılın
doğru	götürebileceği	sınırlılık	
eskiydi	mağara	tamamen	

(Adapted from *Televizyon: Öldüren Eğlence* translated by Osman Akinhay – the Turkish translation of Neil Postman's *Amusing Ourselves to Death*)

Cloze activity with a clearly defined purpose

Objective: Selecting the appropriate connective.

Task: Working in pairs, choose the right joining word from the box below to fill in the gaps in the passage.

and	so	so that	but
when	because	then	

I'll never forget how I felt when I first moved to this country. I came to Britain _____ my father _____ brother were already living here. My father came over first _____ he could find a job and somewhere to live. _____ my brother came six months later _____ he was old enough to work. He started to work in my father's restaurant _____ he could earn enough to send back money to poor mother.

_____ after two and a half years _____ he had sent enough money, we packed our things and prepared to leave. I was very excited _____ I wanted us all to be together again. _____ I also knew that I would miss my cousins, aunts and uncles. _____ we promised that we would write _____ send photos of our new lives.

_____ we arrived we felt very strange _____ everything was so different, _____ my brother had changed so much. _____ a while we got used to everything. It was wonderful to be with my father _____ brother again.

Dolphins

Into The Blue

Of the thirty-odd species of oceanic Dolphin none makes a more striking entrance than Stenella attenuata the spotted dolphin. Under water spotted dolphins first app as white dots against the Blue. The beaks of the adults are white-tipped and that distinctive blaze viewed head-on makes a perfect circle. When the vanguard of School is "echolocating" on you - examining you soncally - the beaks all swing your way. and each circular blaze reflects light before any of the rest of the animal. Close. you see spots Befor your eyes.

(from *Extending Literacy* by David Wray and Maureen Lewis)

Directed Activities Related to Texts (DARTs)

The tendency for teachers to focus on readability, and therefore to simplify texts so that children can read them unaided, can produce very unchallenging work. In the words of Alison Littlefair, 'Simplifying more difficult texts by producing worksheets may ease problems initially but, by doing this, we are not grappling with the task of teaching children to read (and write) a range of texts'. It is worth remembering that if the teacher reads the text to the class in a positive manner, including modelling how to read it, the text selected can be a much more difficult one than the students may be able to access unaided. Shared reading needs to include the thinking process. Teachers often show how to do things, but they also need to articulate the thinking process that underlies the action, for example, discussing how to use context to cope with difficult words.

One of the best solutions to the problem is devising ways of presenting the text that help students access to it and avoid copying. The acronym often used to describe these activities is DARTs. There is a list of DARTs on Template 29, page 57.

Providing support for reading and writing

Directed Activities Related to Texts were first developed and given this acronym in the 1970s. Their purpose is to help students make sense of texts in ways that are far more constructive and interesting than using simplified texts, setting decontextualised comprehension exercises or copying. They also often help to focus the work at a suitable conceptual level, as the way the students are involved in the learning process helps them to understand the nature of what is being considered. This not only supports their reading, but aids their ability to construct similar text. Obviously no process is guaranteed to be effective. The effectiveness of DARTs is dependent on matching the activity to the objective of the lesson and the learning needs of the students. The text selected should be challenging but within the capacity of the group using it. This may require differentiating the texts selected for different groups.

Resources

A book that develops the thinking behind these activities and takes you through the practical processes involved is *Extending Literacy – children reading and writing non-fiction* (David Wray and Maureen Lewis, see page 141 for more details). This superb book looks at how well children's skills are extended once they have achieved basic literacy, and focuses on practical approaches to extending literacy using non-fiction texts. All the examples are from primary lessons right across the curriculum, but the processes outlined are applicable at secondary level and beyond. Several of the following examples are taken from this book, which is highly recommend. Other useful resource books are: *Use of Language Across the Secondary Curriculum* by Eve Bearne, *Analytical and DiscursiveWriting at Key Stage 3* by Christine Counsell, *Breakthrough to Learning, Linguistics in the Service of Mainstream Education* by Mary Mason and Bob Mason (see Appendix 7, page 142 for more details).

Presenter's notes

Templates 30–33 (pages 58–61) are illustrations of a variety of DARTs that could be used in a training session dedicated to DARTs' techniques. Use Template 29, page 57 to explain some of the processes involved. The list is divided into three sections:

☐ The structure of texts
☐ Interrogating and transforming texts
☐ Seeing the big picture

Some of the suggestions are further explained below.

The structure of texts

Sequencing

This is the name given to the process of ordering cut-up sections of text to establish meaning through structuring the text appropriately. It is an excellent way of focusing attention on text. It normally results in high levels of concentration and vigorous discussion as students strive to solve the puzzle and establish the logic of how to order the text sensibly. The discussion this involves is central to the process. Any ensuing work related to the text will be greatly enhanced by this discussion. The text selected for sequencing on Template 30, page 58, from Daniel Pennac's *Reads Like a Novel*, is suitable for adults. The paragraphs are presented in the wrong order so that it is ready for use as a sequencing exercise for staff. The actual paragraph order is as follows: D, O, A, M, P, F.

I would suggest using this text as a sequencing exercise for staff on a training day to show or remind them of the power of this process.

Some practical tips on sequencing:

☐ Select a really good text that will expand the group's horizons but is not beyond their reach
☐ Scan or type the text into a word processor
☐ Reorder the paragraphs before cutting up the text – this prevents students from being able to reassemble the text using the logic of a jigsaw rather than structure and content
☐ Give each paragraph some sort of coded title if you wish to be able to identify specific paragraphs in later discussion.

Cloze passages

This is the name given to text where some key words have been deleted. A good cloze passage should have blanks that have been carefully selected to enhance the purpose of the lesson. Cloze passages are most constructive if part of paired activity, since it is the discussion around the possible choices that maximises the learning process. They can be made easier by giving students a possible choice of words to fill the gaps, but there should be more words than spaces and no hint should be given as to the opening letter of the words or the number of letters they contain.

Interrogating and transforming texts

Transformation

This involves students presenting in a different form some of the information they have read, by selecting material appropriate to the purpose and audience of the task.

Presenter's notes

For example, show the staff the advert for scribes on Template 31, page 59. Explain that the class had been presented with a range of information about ancient Egypt and then given the task of writing an advert for scribes. Given the nature of the task, they could not copy from the text but had to select appropriate information and restructure it according to the nature of the task. Explain that the boy has managed to transform a piece of historical writing into an interesting yet factually accurate advert that would have been entertaining to write. Read out the bottom paragraph of the advert to illustrate this point.

Flow charts

A variant of this restructuring is to select a text that lends itself to diagrammatic representation and then ask the class to transform the information from the text accordingly.

Presenter's notes

Point out that the example on Template 32, page 60 is particularly interesting since the six-year-old child who completed this life cycle of the duck could not read the passage unaided but could understand its content when it was read to her, and was thus able to sum up its content in a flow diagram. Point out that if a six-year-old child can manage to represent a biological process so successfully in flow diagram form, there will be many possibilities within the secondary curriculum for students to transform text in such a manner.

Seeing the big picture

Jigsaws

These are a superb device for using feedback from groups to help the whole class gain an understanding of the big picture. Jigsaws lend themselves to a wide range of humanities areas as well as to any subject where you need to consider what the parts contribute to the whole, e.g. when studying the body, or global warming as in the example on Template 33, page 61. This is organised in the following way:

☐ Divide a topic up into batches of information
☐ Divide your class into the same number of groups and allocate each one a different batch of information
☐ Ask the students in these groups, within a specific time frame, each to research one aspect of their information and discuss their findings together so that they are all aware of the key points
☐ Create different groups consisting of one representative from each of the information groups
☐ Each group member in turn explains the findings of their previous group so that, by using each other's expertise, each group can piece together the whole picture
☐ Alternatively, each original group could report back to the whole class.

You can, of course, deliberately set up a group that does not quite fit the picture but is relevant since it is a possible solution rather than a cause. For example, when studying global warming, as on Template 33, page 61, you could create a seventh group that looked at renewable energy: wind, waves, water, etc. This approach works as well with 11-year-olds as with sixth-formers or adults. It is a question of ensuring that the topic in question and the material available are of a level suited to the researchers.

The relevance game

This is an activity based on group discussion.

Preparation:
☐ Write various facts relating to the topic being taught on to pieces of card
☐ Select an essay title or task relating to the topic
☐ Divide the class into groups giving each the task/essay title and a set of cards.

How to play:
☐ Discuss the various facts on the cards
☐ Select those that are relevant to the task
☐ Discard those which are not relevant
☐ Work out how to justify your choices.

Example: The illustration that Christine Counsell uses in *Analytical and Discursive Writing at Key Stage 3* is a series of cards containing facts relating to the great fire of London. The question the children are focusing on is 'Why did the great fire of London (1666) get out of control and destroy so much of London?'

The cards should be devised so that some are relevant to the question, and others relate to the topic but not to the question asked. The children then have to discuss which cards to select as relevant and discard those that are not. For example, 'Someone started a fire in Pudding Lane' should be relegated to the irrelevant pile, whereas 'The houses in London were built very close together' should be selected as relevant.

Such a process can be adapted to suit students of all ages and abilities. The *KS3 Literacy Conferences Video* (DfEE) contains a useful section from a geography lesson in Thomas Tallis School on this approach and how it can be developed.

Grids and frames

Grids and frames can be an excellent way of developing thinking and structuring ideas. They are discussed in more detail on pages 62–70.

Directed Activities Related to non-fiction Texts (DARTs)

These activities are designed to help students make sense of texts and come to realise, in a constructive way, the processes underlying the structure of texts. Key to the success of most of these activities is their collaborative nature, which encourages students to interrogate and reflect on text.

Questions to consider when selecting the most appropriate activities:

☐ Are you seeking to help the students consider the structure of the text?

☐ Are you seeking to help the students select relevant information from text?

☐ Are you seeking to help the students confront the complexity of a range of text or information?

The unit planning grid on Template 62 might also be useful at this point.

The structure of text

☐ **Sequencing** Students have to order cut-up sections of text to establish meaning through structuring the text appropriately. The discussion this involves is essential (see Template 30).

☐ **Cloze** In pairs, students decide which words would fill the gaps in a passage. The deleted words should be carefully chosen according to the purpose of the exercise. Discussion is essential. The chosen words should fit the grammar, sense and style of the original (see Template 27).

☐ **Prediction/reconstruction** Class or groups play 'Sherlock Holmes' and hypothesise and construct a text from its opening/closing paragraphs by analysing and reflecting on what they have read. Later they compare their predictions with the original full text.

☐ **Structure/boundaries** In groups, students are asked to divide a text into sections by establishing what distinguishes one section of the text from another.

☐ **Substitution** Students are given a text in which some words or phrases, indicated by a different typeface, have been replaced by less effective alternatives. In pairs, students decide what words they would replace them with and why their chosen words are an improvement.

Interrogating or transforming texts

☐ **Transformation** Students have to present the text in a different form or genre (e.g. as a newspaper article, a police report, an advert, a poster, a radio report, instructions etc.). This involves selecting and presenting information for a different, specified audience (see Template 31). Such a task may need a writing frame to support it.

☐ **Open-ended questions** A few challenging questions are set for which the text offers no obvious single correct answer. Students have to consider the full text to deduce their answers. The reasons for coming to their decision are central to group feedback on the answers.

☐ **Flowcharts/diagrams/drawings** Students are asked to make a visual representation of some of the information in a text (see Template 32). This often benefits from being a paired activity.

☐ **Interrogation** In groups, students formulate the questions that need to be answered in order to understand the text.

☐ **Highlighting text** Students are asked to highlight or annotate parts of a text that relate to particular issues or aspects. This often benefits from being a paired activity.

☐ **Statement game** Students are presented with a short choice of statements that supposedly sum up the text, some of which are inappropriate. In pairs or groups the students decide which one or ones are the most apt and why.

☐ **Summary** Students select the key points of a text and express them as briefly and clearly as possible. Highlighting text and the statement game can be useful introductory activities here.

Seeing the big picture

☐ **Jigsaws** Students research one aspect of a topic in groups and then come together in different groupings to piece together the whole picture (see Template 33).

☐ **Relevance game** Write key facts relating to an issue on pieces of card. In groups, students have to decide which cards are relevant given particular questions, and explain their selection.

☐ **KWL/prior knowledge research grids** 'What do I **k**now?', 'What do I **w**ant to know?', 'What have I **l**earnt?' grids help students recognise what they already know about a topic before embarking on it, as well as beginning to plan what is to be investigated. The grids also inform the teacher about the extent of the students' prior knowledge on the topic (see Template 34).

☐ **Planning frames** Such frames provide a structure for a task. For example, a comparison grid would help students compare one concept, artefact or text with another. This could be in preparation for an essay or a discussion (see Template 35). Further examples of planning frames are on Templates 39 and 47.

☐ **Thinking Frames** These grids or frames help students to think about and then make notes on the key aspects of the text topic focused on. The essential point is to use the grid to oblige students to consider difficult concepts that may otherwise be overlooked (see Templates 37–40).

Sequencing

Daniel Pennac's *Reads Like a Novel*, Chapter 32

Reads Like a Novel was the number one bestseller in France in 1993. It is a fascinating book about the need for schools to teach the love of reading, as well as teaching reading itself.

Activity

Section 0   Of course, a case can be made for this.
There's no shortage of arguments.

Section M   It's a matter of luck, and no thanks to the greatness of the institution, if a student, from time to time, meets a teacher who is enthusiastic enough to consider mathematics in their own right. Imparting maths as if they were Fine Arts, the teacher inspires a love for them by virtue of his own vitality, and thanks to him effort is turned into pleasure.

Section A   A school cannot be a school for pleasure, since pleasure depends closely on one's being disinterested and free. A school is necessarily a place where knowledge is manufactured, and knowledge requires effort. The subjects taught there are the tools of consciousness. The teachers responsible for these subjects are initiators. They can't be expected to eulogise disinterested intellectual learning, when everything, absolutely everything in school life – curricula, marks, exams, league-tables, levels of degree, subjects, specialisations – stresses the competitive goal of the institution, a goal itself determined by the labour market.

Section D   It's depressing, all the same, this consensus. It's as if, from the remarks of Rousseau on learning to read, to those of Klaus Mann on the teaching of literature by the Bavarian State, via the irony of the schoolmaster's young wife, ending with the lamentations of the students of here and now, the role of school has been restricted everywhere and for ever to the teachings of techniques, and the need for commentary. It's as if school has cut off direct access to books by outlawing the pleasure of reading. It seems to be established for all time, world-wide, that there's no place for pleasure in the school curriculum, and that knowledge can be gained only as the fruit of properly understood suffering.

Section F   Functionality rules here.
Life is elsewhere.

Section P   It's the prerogative of living things to inspire a love for life, even in the form of a quadratic equation; but vitality has never been part of the school curriculum.

⚑ SCRIBES WANTED ⚑

Apprentices are needed to train as Scribes. Training takes 5 years. In that time you will

- learn the 700 writing signs
- practise writing
- copy letters, documents, acounts and stories
- pratise division and number problems

When qualified you will

- collect taxes
- keep the records/taccounts
- record animals in tax counts

Sons of scribes are invited to apply for this job. Sons of farmers and workers cannot apply. Training will take place in the House of life. Apply to the Inspector of ~~Acoounts~~ Scribes. Eygpt.

(from Extending Literacy – children reading and writing non-fiction by David Wray and Maureen Lewis)

Flow chart

The life cycle of a duck by a Year 2 child

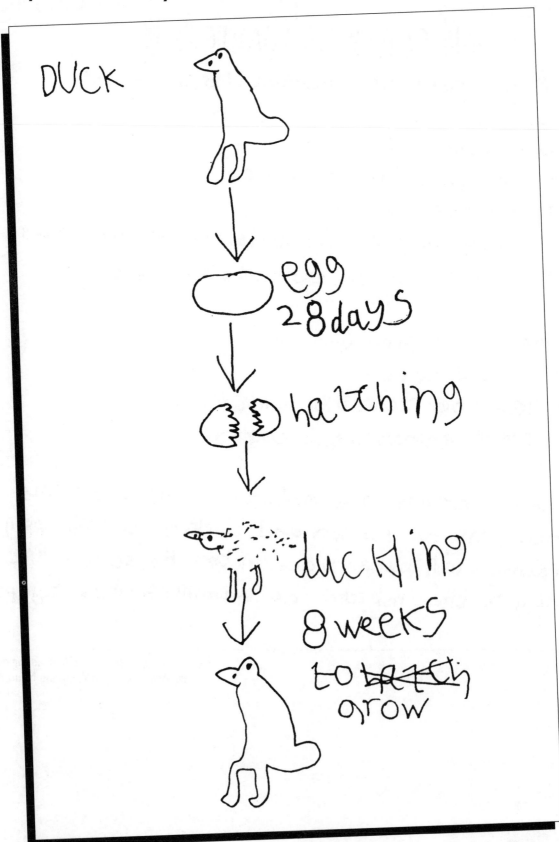

DUCK

egg
28days

hatching

duckling
8 weeks
to ~~hatch~~ grow

(from *Extending Literacy – children reading and writing
non-fiction* by David Wray and Maureen Lewis)

The jigsaw approach

Global warming – what will happen if CO_2 levels rise?

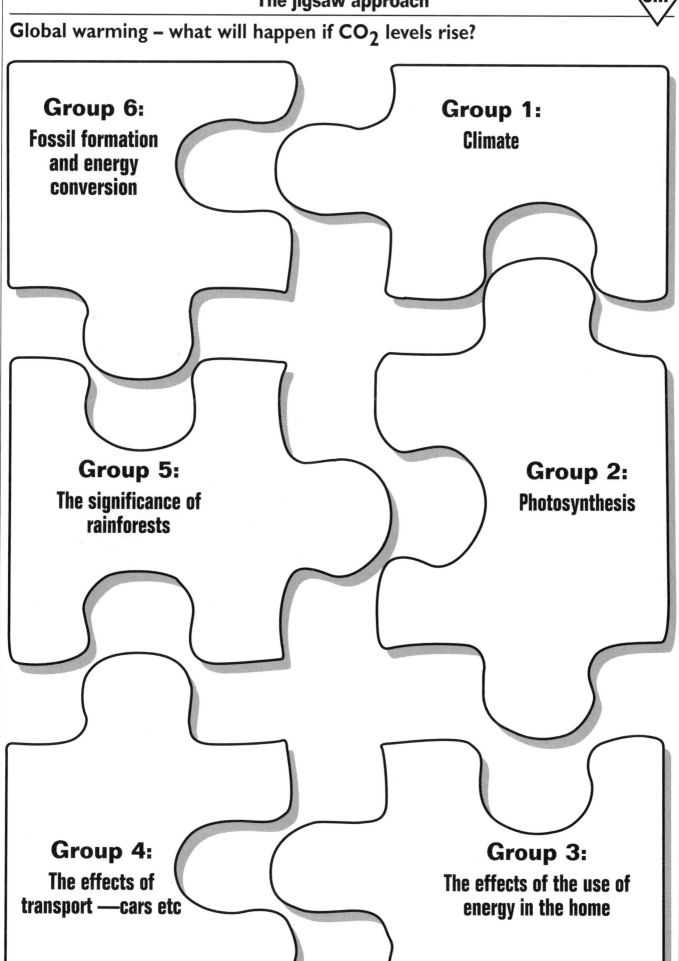

Group 6:
Fossil formation and energy conversion

Group 1:
Climate

Group 5:
The significance of rainforests

Group 2:
Photosynthesis

Group 4:
The effects of transport —cars etc

Group 3:
The effects of the use of energy in the home

Using grids and frames

Grids or frames are a device that has been used by teachers in various forms for decades. In recent years their use has become more systematic as a means of supporting student learning. Below is a short summary of the various types of frames and grids to help clarify their meaning and uses. This section deals with the first three types. Speaking frames and writing frames are dealt with in the following two sections.

Activating prior knowledge (KWL) grids

These are a form of planning frame that helps the students to recognise what they already know about a topic before embarking on it, as well as beginning to establish what is to be investigated. They also inform the teacher as to the extent of the students' prior knowledge on the subject.

Planning frames

These help students to structure their ideas before attempting more difficult related work. **Discussion grids** and **comparison grids** fall into this category.

Thinking frames

These focus on helping students to think about the key elements underlying a unit of work or extended text. They help students to grasp the big picture.

Writing frames

These provide not just the structure for an extended piece of writing, but the opening words of each significant paragraph. They support students in writing in unfamiliar or more complex genres. Writing frames are discussed in more detail on pages 79–95.

Speaking frames

These similarly provide the structure and the opening phrases for significant parts of a possible speech. They support students in speaking in unfamiliar registers. Speaking frames are discussed in more detail on page 73. See also Template 72, page 114.

All of these frames should be introduced as follows if the teachers are to encourage the students to become independent learners. The teacher first models the process through explanation and demonstration, then jointly completes the frame with the class as a shared activity. The students are then in a position to work effectively using the frame to support their thinking, planning, writing or speaking. The students should then be involved in creating their own frames so that they become familiar with the process and are in a position to work independently of the frame, having internalised the process. This teaching model is illustrated on Template 51, page 87.

Presenter's notes
Prior knowledge/KWL grids

Extending Literacy (see Appendix 7, page 141) provides detailed explanations of why the KWL grid on Template 34, page 64 is a useful tool for beginning a new topic, since it is based on establishing what the student already knows about the subject. This helps the student to build on existing knowledge and enables the teacher to establish where the student is starting from and whether they are have any serious misconceptions relating to the topic. The first column allows the student to list what they already know, which may or not be accurate, like the statement 'They lived in straw houses' in the example on Template 34, page 64. The central column, 'What do I want to know?', can be determined by the teacher or the student, though at some stage all students need to be able to ask the right sort of questions to maximise the effectiveness of their research. The final column, 'What have I learnt?', encourages the child to sum up the essence of what has been discovered, while discouraging the copying of large chunks of text.

Planning/discussion grids

Grids or frames can be a very useful way of focusing students' thinking and discussion. They are a very versatile tool, for example, comparison grids are an excellent way to encourage students to think about the similarities and differences between two aspects of a topic (see Template 35, page 65). These can be in preparation for a discursive essay, but they are equally useful in helping to focus thinking or build up vocabulary. This can be a good way of involving students in the process of selecting the most appropriate vocabulary.

Presenter's notes

The more students are involved in building up the information for a topic, the more effective it will be. For example, the comparison grid could contain the names of two portraits by different artists plus, down the side, a list of features that need to be considered for each painting, as in the example on Template 35, page 65.

☐ Students work in pairs. Each pair has a copy of a portrait by Van Gogh and a portrait by Picasso.

☐ Each pair discusses which words best sum up the characteristics in the grid for each artist.

☐ The whole class then discusses the topic – the best terms are written on the board.

☐ This could then become a wall chart to support the vocabulary for this particular unit of work.

In this way the class is involved in the process of developing the appropriate vocabulary rather than passively being told the words. This makes the learning process more meaningful.

Another example of a planning frame is given on Template 36, page 66. This frame helps groups devise a dramatic scene. It serves as a reminder of the key issues relating to plot and character and provides a scaffold to support planning.

Thinking frames

Grids can be developed into thinking frames to help students develop and structure their thinking. They can be used to sum up the essence of a unit or text. In particular they are excellent for helping students to grasp the big picture and apply information learnt in one context to a range of situations.

To demonstrate how this simple device can help focus thinking appropriately, consider what is involved when filling in a job application and preparing for an interview. By definition, a new job tends to be new territory, so applicants have to demonstrate how their existing experience and ideas make them suitable for the post. However, in reality many very literate applicants do not do this and write their supporting statement as some form of chronological account of what they've done so far, rather than focusing on the specification of the new job. Equally, many candidates in interview do not shift their knowledge from the territory that is familiar to them to the new ground that is the territory of the post they are hoping to fill.

Presenter's notes

Use the interview frame on Template 37, page 67, to show how the simple device of a thinking frame can help focus both writing the statement and preparing appropriately for an interview. Talk staff through the following process:

☐ In the left-hand column list the job specification to remind you what the employer is looking for

☐ Use the middle column to sum up the key points that demonstrate how your experience has prepared you for the post

☐ Use the final column to jot down how you would develop the post.

Structuring your written application is now easy, since you take each aspect of the job specification in turn and show how you fit it and how you would develop it. When it comes to the interview you have already shifted your thinking into the employer's territory.

In the same way that candidates tend to avoid the tricky territory of the new ground and cling to the security of what they already know, students in school try to avoid difficult territory. But it is grasping this territory that makes learning interesting and often allows students to start to understand the subject. Moreover, it is this territory that divides mediocre exam grades from good exam grades. Central to constructing useful thinking frames is deciding what is the tricky area (watershed) within any topic or subject area and ensuring that you include columns that force students (and teachers) to start thinking about it. To illustrate this for staff, look at the thinking frame on Template 38, page 68, which was constructed to provide a framework for understanding the structure of any play.

The first three columns are straightforward. At A-Level English a student who could only write about a text, however accurately, within the confines of these first three columns would, at best, get a D grade. It is the next column, 'Writer's dramatic purpose', that is the watershed. Deciding what to put in this column is much more difficult and should be the source of much useful discussion. Students need to be able to write in this mode if they are to start to produce interesting analytical essays that can achieve good grades. Teachers will find that having to consider this question for every section of a play also enhances their own understanding of the text. Thus, a well-constructed thinking frame helps to move the thinking of the students and the teacher up a gear or two.

Involving the students

Handing students a completed grid like that on Template 39, page 69 would be a complete waste of time. They must be involved in the process as follows:

☐ First, discuss the particular issue/section with the group

☐ Next, the students complete the grid

☐ Then their findings are discussed jointly and a content is agreed that is an amalgamation of the best thoughts of the group

☐ Type this up for the whole group to use (obviously students can adapt this in the light of their own thinking).

A further advantage of such an approach is that it condenses a significant amount of information on to an easy-to-assimilate sheet that can easily be added to as your thoughts develop, and that is excellent for revising from. Too many students end up with thick folders of notes that they painfully attempt to revise. Thinking through the information on sheets like this leads to much more focused and effective revision because it is centred on focused and effective thought. It means that whatever question is asked in the exam, the students are likely to have sufficiently ordered thoughts to be in a good position to adapt their knowledge to answer effectively the question asked.

Not all columns need be completed on a first discussion. The final two, for example, could be left to a later date, as in the *Anthony and Cleopatra* example on Template 39, page 69.

Thinking frames like these can be developed at a variety of levels to support a wide range of subjects, as in Templates 38 and 40, pages 68 and 70 respectively. The idea is to decide what the tricky areas of a unit are that students will tend to avoid unless they are forced to confront them. Template 36, page 66 breaks down a dramatic scene into all its compeonent parts, starting with more general elements in 1 and adding detail about characters in 2. In this way students will not neglect any of the important elements of the scene.

In Example 1 on Template 40, page 70, the grid forces students to consider not only the specific function of a part of a body or plant, but its special features. In the more complicated example from economics, the grid focuses students on considering the essence of specific economic issues. Students will not be able to consider the comparisons or complexities column if they have not grasped the key aspects of the issue under consideration.

Ask staff to consider what is the trickiest aspect of a particular unit and see if constructing a grid would help students to begin to tackle this.

Template 60, page 96, shows how DARTs, including grids and frames, can be relevant across every area of the curriculum.

Activating prior knowledge – KWL grid

Vikings

What do I know?	What do I want to know?	What have I learnt?
They had wars.	Why did they sail all over England?	
They had maps.	Why did they have longships?	
They had dogs.	Why did they have dogs?	
They had longships.		
They lived in straw houses.		
They had fleas.		
They had helmets.		
They sailed all over England.		
They had shields.		

(from *Extending Literacy – children reading and writing non-fiction* by David Wray and Maureen Lewis)

Comparison grid (used as a discussion grid)

To support discussion or planning for essay writing (report genre)

The grid below has been devised to help structure a paired discussion in art, comparing the techniques of two artists, with the aim of building up students' observation and understanding of technique supported by the appropriate vocabulary. Each pair has a portrait by Picasso and a portrait by Van Gogh.

Instructions

☐ List in column 1 the characteristics to be considered.

☐ In the columns numbered 2 and 3, put the names of the items/concepts being compared or contrasted.

1 Characteristics	2 Portrait by Van Gogh	3 Portrait by Picasso
Use of light		
Use of colour		
Texture		
Level of realism		
Context		
Mood		
Impression of character		

Note: This grid could be used for pair work before a whole-group discussion. A grid of the most appropriate vocabulary could then be built up on the board. This could form the basis for a wall poster to support the unit of work. This involves the students in the process of developing their vocabulary.

Planning frame for dramatic scenes. Title _____

1 Initial planning

Message	Setting	Opening hook	Key events	Dramatic techniques	Finale

2 Characters

Characters	Appearance, personality	Language, tone/voice	Movement, gesture, expression	Role/purpose	Props

Thinking frame for job interview

How you will develop the post	How your experience fulfils the specification	Job specification

Thinking frame for plays: synopsis of _____

OHP

Act	Location and key characters	Central events	Writer's dramatic purpose	Key quotes	Imagery	Themes

A thinking frame to develop a synopsis of *Anthony and Cleopatra*

ACT	Location	Key Characters	Central Events	Writer's Dramatic Purpose	Key Quotes	Imagery	Themes
I.i	Egypt, Cleo's palace	Philo Demetrius – never reappear A and C and train	Philo intros A and C to audience from Roman viewpoint: A as great general sunk to doting fool. A spurns messenger from Rome. Will never leave Egypt.	To intro A and C to audience from Roman viewpoint. Audience to get strong visual image of glory and decadence of A and C's lifestyle.	But this dotage of our generals. – Let Rome in Tiber melt...		
I.ii	Egypt	C's women and soothsayer – Enobarbus + Cleopatra + Antony	Sexual gossip, punning and fortune telling – A hears news of wife's wars – decides to leave Egypt. Then news that wife dead. – Further resolves to leave. Reviles Cleo but Enobarbus praises her.	Create series of clashing images. contrast Egypt with Rome. Pressure on A to leave but constant lure of C. Visually and thematically ever changing. Shows A determining to leave.	These strong Egyptian fetters – must from the enchanting... You had then...		
I.iii	Egypt	Cleo + ladies + Antony	C planning false moods to beguile A. C's playacting interrupted by A's determination to leave; C feigns fainting fit then instantly recovers.	Shows C's guiles and A's dilemma torn between duty and personal pleasure.	The strong necessity of time... I am quickly ill...		
I.iv	Rome, Caesar's house	Caesar, Lepidus and messengers	Caesar decrying A's voluptuousness/indulgence. Hears news of Pompey's revolt. Needs A to return, recalls his magnificent soldiership.	Short scene to show Roman viewpoint and intro's Caesar. Intro's political threat and Caesar's need of A. Shows his genuine admiration of A at his heroic best. Shows Lepidus is weak and Caesar is in control and always plotting/rational.	He fishes, drinks and wastes the lamps of night in revel... A, leave thy lascivious wassails...		
I.v	Egypt, C's palace	Cleo and attendants	C indulging in sexy jokes with attendants. Bemoaning A's departure. Servant suggests she equally missed Julius Caesar. C denies this. Determines to send endless messengers to A.	Contrasting scene: sensual and relaxing. C missing A but excess of emotion, irrational. Strictly personal but is it real love or playacting?	The demi-Atlas of this earth... He shall hath every day a several greeting.		
2.i	Messina, Sicily, Pompey's house	Pompey and Menas	Pompey determined to challenge triumvirate's control of empire. Hears of A's return to Rome because of his threat. Is flattered by this.	Shows external threat – man of action, potential threat. Need for vigilance if to maintain control of empire. Therefore can't afford A – must be singleminded.	His soldiership is twice the other twain... The people love me and the sea...		

Developing thinking frames

Thinking frames can be developed to help at a range of levels. They could be used to help build up the appropriate vocabulary for a unit of work, as in the biology example below.

Example 1

Vocabulary thinking grid for a unit of work in Biology

Word	Location	Function	Special features

Or, at a more complex level, they could be used to try to help students to understand a whole range of different concepts relating to a particular subject area, as in the economics example below.

Example 2

Thinking frame for Economics

Topic	Brief summary	Key concepts	Comparisons	Complexities	Key examples

The language of learning

Being able to speak a word or phrase confidently or express an idea coherently is a crucial foundation for using the language and ideas of learning appropriately when writing, or for understanding them when reading. Every curriculum area is dependent on the spoken word. All teachers need to consider the language and concepts of every unit of work – how lessons can be planned, not only to help students become familiar and confident with the language of the unit, but also to aid them in internalising the concepts and related processes underpinning the unit. The list on Template 41, page 74, suggests some ways of doing this.

Teaching key vocabulary

All teachers need to build up lists of the key words that are to be covered in a topic. A central question is, what to do with these lists once you have them. Putting them up on the wall is all very well, but they can too often become wallpaper and, unless they are an integral part of lesson planning, will not become part of the children's vocabulary.

Some schools ensure that each child has a vocabulary book in which to write words, adding to the list in every lesson. The trouble with this is that it has a tendency to become highly bureaucratic. Moreover, the emphasis here is on the student copying down long lists of decontextualised words and their definitions, which may never be assimilated in practice. 'Naming is not knowing', as Liz Mellor, Senior Lecturer in Music at Homerton College, has so aptly put it in *Use of language across the secondary curriculum* (Routledge). There is much to be said for focusing activity on using the words in context and talking through how they are used in practice, rather than on writing the words down in endless lists.

Presenter's notes

A good way of making teachers more aware of the need to get children to hear, see, read, write and speak the language of any unit is to show the errors from the KS2 science SATS on Template 42, page 75. Apparently some children, after their first day of the literacy hour, went home complaining that they'd waited all day but hadn't received any liquorice. We all have a tendency to turn unfamiliar words into words that we know, without realising our mistake. For example, I spent years assuming that hang gliding was hand gliding. So we have to teach in a way that minimises this problem. If children see a word written and use the word in context, they are more likely to build up their confidence with the term and, in effect, add it to their vocabulary. Further guidance on some of the activities listed in Template 41, page 74, is given below.

Modelling the thinking process

Undoubtedly, being able to talk through a process helps to fix that process in your mind and reveals gaps in your understanding.

As teachers, we have all experienced the ghastly moment when, in full flood of explanation, you realise that you haven't fully understood the process and don't quite know where it goes next. Though not an ideal position to find yourself in, it is a useful reminder of just how important talking through a process is to having a full understanding of it. This needs to be built into the planning of lessons so that students have plenty of opportunities to do this in a variety of forms.

Use the extract from a TES article on Template 43, page 76 and/or the text on Template 44, page 77 (from an unknown source) to illustrate modelling the thinking process.

Reviewing the lesson

Students reviewing the lesson, which is an integral part of the literacy hour, is an excellent model to follow. All teachers should be encouraged to build this into their planning. It helps to build structure and purpose into lessons and to involve students in the learning process.

It is also a way of involving students who have not been taking part in the practical activities, but have been present for all the explanation and have witnessed others participating. For example, those who, for whatever reason, are not participating in PE lessons, could be required to explain the key points of the lesson along with those who have participated.

Establishing current vocabulary

Brainstorming words to establish what a class already knows is all very well, but it only really tells you what some individuals know – the majority may not have the faintest idea.

When beginning a unit of work or text with significant potentially new vocabulary, one way of establishing just how much of the key vocabulary individuals already know is by producing a list of the words, providing every student with a copy, and reading the list to the class.
The students mark up the list as follows:

x = never heard of word

? = heard of word but uncertain of meaning

✓ = know what it means – ticks should be accompanied by attempted explanation of meaning (this can be made easier by providing multiple choice options for each word).

This process can be attempted again at the end of a unit to establish what has been learnt.

Video commentary

An extension of the role play is video commentary, where video is used to enable students to make commentaries on the performance of others. For example, in Little Ilford School, Newham, London, students scripted commentary using appropriate vocabulary and then filmed a gymnastics performance while commentating. Playing back the video enabled the class to evaluate both the activity and the commentary.

Word and concept games

There is a vast range of imaginative ways in which children can be involved in using the key vocabulary of a unit in context. Here are just four:

☐ Dominoes

☐ Bingo

☐ Splat

☐ Twenty questions

All four require the children to have already been introduced to the key words/concepts in context. All of the games reinforce the children's understanding of the terms. Dominoes and Twenty questions require the most thought and oral participation. Twenty questions is particularly good for developing questioning and listening skills.

Dominoes

Key words are written on dominoes as Template 73, page 115. (All the words in this example form part of the technical language of the literacy hour, and are included here as the target vocabulary of a Year 7 unit of work that builds on the literacy hour framework for students in English primary schools in Year 6.) The idea initially is to see if pairs of children can set all of their dominoes in a straight line – in order to put a word down, they have to be able to explain the logical link between the words or concepts, as in the example below.

If a child has put down 'imperative' next to 'verb', this could be justified by explaining that, when the type of verb being used is an instruction, this is known as the imperative.

Dominoes is easily adapted to all areas of the curriculum. For example, if you were teaching PE, you could devise a game of dominoes to cover the rules of each game, as in the football dominoes below. Teachers of practical lessons may prefer to stick with word games like 'Splat', explained below, since these can be done with only a board and therefore lend themselves to spaces like a gymnasium.

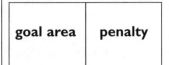 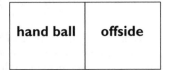

When making your dominoes it is best to make them reversible so that hand ball/offside, when turned over, reads offside/hand ball. In this way the words can always be used the right way up.

Once children have got the hang of this, they can play the game proper dominoes-style, when each would have an equal number of dominoes and would try to win by using all of his or her dominoes first. You may always want the game to be played collaboratively since this encourages meaningful discussion. Competition could be provided by seeing which pair or group is the first to finish. This activity can vary in difficulty depending on the level of the words chosen.

The process can be reviewed by asking one pair of children to talk through the links they have made. If you have a fuzzy felt board, this makes the process easier to illustrate. Make large versions of the word dominoes that can be stuck on the felt board. The students rearrange the dominoes to show what links they made. They explain each link. The class then comments on the validity of each explanation.

Using dominoes in a training session

It is a good idea for staff to play word dominoes as part of a training session. Playing it makes you realise what a thorough knowledge of the vocabulary you need in order to be able to play effectively. You can print the dominoes on Template 73, page 115 on to card (printing them in reverse fashion on the back if possible) and then cut the pages up into the separate dominoes. Put each complete set into an envelope – you will need one set per two or three members of staff.

Bingo

Using approximately 20 key words/concepts from a unit, create bingo cards, each card showing a different selection of 10 of the 20 words (see Template 45, page 78). You then give simple definitions of one word at a time. The students can tick off a word if it matches the definition. A prize can be allotted to the winner once their selection has been verified. You can make this more difficult by asking a student to be the caller, but only providing them with the words, not the definitions.

Splat

(This was graphically illustrated at a lecture given by Maureen Lewis at the NAAE conference on 20th March 1999.)
☐ Write 10 key words on the board
☐ Divide the class into two teams and provide a representative of each team with a fly swat
☐ Before commencing play, make the rules clear:
  – Only one splat allowed per word
  – Splatting each other is not allowed
  – Teams must not call out
☐ Say a definition of one of the words on the board
☐ The first representative to splat the appropriate word wins a point for their team.

The game can be made more interesting if a member from each team is required to provide the definitions. They would lose a point for their team if the definition they provided was inadequate (referee's decision is final).

Be aware that the highly competitive nature of this game could lend itself to certain students being ridiculed. Care should be taken when deciding which groups to play this with. Template 45, page 78 gives examples of Splat/Bingo Maths and Music style.

Twenty questions

(My thanks to Peter Hoskins, biology teacher from Bishopstone School, Swansea, for including this at the plenary session of a training day on literacy across the curriculum.)

Preparation:
☐ Write the key names of objects relating to the topic on to cards (one card per word/concept)
☐ Divide the class into pairs with a few cards per pair, face down.

Rules:
☐ The partner can only answer 'Yes' or 'No' to questions asked by the card holder.

How to play:
☐ Students take turns holding a card to their forehead and asking pertinent questions of their partner to establish which card they are holding. They have a maximum of 20 questions.
☐ As soon as a questioner guesses a card correctly the roles are reversed.

This process demands significant thinking and speaking skills on behalf of the questioners if they are to establish who or what they are.

Precise instructions

Most of us use language rather imprecisely, but some subjects, like Mathematics, rely on a very precise use of language. One way to help children use terms appropriately is to ask one person to describe a process while another follows the instructions exactly. 'How to crack an egg' can be very entertaining but tends to entail a lot of clearing up. A safer option is noughts and crosses.

☐ Ask a student to explain, without using a diagram, how to draw a noughts and crosses grid.
☐ Follow the instructions precisely on the board.
☐ Ask other members of the class to amend the instructions until the grid is correct.

This is much more exacting than it sounds. This game can be adapted to suit the contents of a wide range of subjects and is particularly relevant for Maths.

Speaking frames

What and how you write should be dependent on audience and purpose, as should what register you speak in. Many students need help in speaking outside of the mode or dialect that they are most familiar with. This is not a question of students changing their accent, but of changing the type of words and structures selected to suit whatever the purpose is; in other words, changing their register. Speaking frames are a very useful device to help with this. Students lacking in confidence in formal speaking situations will need the support that such frames can offer.

Speaking frames can provide students with the suitable opening words of each section of a more challenging speaking activity, as well as outlining the content that could be included. Role play is a useful way of getting students to speak in the register appropriate to a variety of roles. For example, a science or geography teacher might wish to engage students in a topic like global warming through role-playing a TV interview on the subject. The students would need support in constructing and presenting an interview involving, for instance, an interviewer, a scientist, a government spokesperson and a representative of Green Peace. The speaking frames could then be linked later on to discussion writing frames to write up the debate, since there are significant links between the formal registers of speaking and writing.

As with writing frames (see pages 79–95), constructing appropriate speaking frames makes the teacher more aware of what is actually involved in the task that the students are being asked to complete. Once students' confidence has been built up through using speaking frames effectively, they could also be involved in the process of planning their own speaking frames, as part of the learning process. This would be especially beneficial for real speaking situations like work experience. This could be linked to constructing the appropriate thinking frame in preparation for an interview (see Template 37, page 67).

An example of a speaking frame is given on Template 72, page 114. In planning where to begin with speaking frames, you need to consider how capable the students are of speaking outside of the register that is most familiar to them, and appropriate support should be given where this proves difficult. In the example on Template 72 registers that are relatively familiar to students, at least through hearing them, if not speaking them, have deliberately been chosen to help build up confidence in these more familiar areas before moving on to more difficult territory. Template 60, page 96 shows how language activities including speaking frames, can be relevant across every curriculum area.

The language of learning

Speaking and listening are central to learning. The following activities and approaches are designed to help students become familiar with the language, concepts and processes involved with units of work. Remember also that discussion is central to the DARTs activities outlined on Template 29.

☐ **Modelling the thinking process** The teacher models the thinking processes that underlie the skills that are being taught. Opportunities are created for students to be involved in explaining out loud these thinking process and issues. This is part of the approach of the National Numeracy Strategy as well as the Literacy Strategy. This process is illustrated on Template 44.

☐ **Reviewing the lesson** This simple mechanism, which is part of modelling the thinking process, has been built into the structure of the literacy hour as the plenary session. At the end of lessons, students explain what they have been doing in relation to the objective of the lesson. This helps students internalise the processes and familiarise themselves with the appropriate language.

☐ **Brainstorming** A brainstorming session is a good way of establishing what information a group already has on a topic. A concluding brainstorm can be a good way of bringing together the knowledge that has been gained through the unit. The smaller the group involved in the brainstorming process, the more everyone is likely to be involved in the process.

☐ **Labelling** Labelling key items of equipment and insisting that their names are used can help students recognise the words when they hear them, and use them appropriately. It also aids spelling.

☐ **Building vocabulary** When beginning a unit you can establish how much of the key vocabulary is new to the students by providing a list of key words that is read to the students. They have to indicate which words they have never heard of, which they have heard of but are unsure of, and which words they know the meaning of. This provides the teacher with useful information on which to plan subsequent vocabulary work.

☐ **Word walls** Establish a space (poster, chart or board) where you can build up a word wall of all the vocabulary of a unit as the words are introduced in context. This strengthens the students' recognition and spelling of the words. The vocabulary should then be integrated into the lesson so students get used to speaking as well as writing them. The plenary session provides excellent opportunities for this (see Template 67).

☐ **Word games**
Dominoes Write the key words/concepts/ of a unit on 'dominoes'. In pairs students have to see if they can place the dominoes in a row, explaining each of the links they have made. This focuses on using the words in context (see Template 73).
Twenty questions Students work in pairs, and take it in turns to hold a card to their forehead and ask pertinent questions of their partner in order to establish which card they are holding. They have a maximum of twenty questions. The partner can only answer Yes or No to the questions asked by the card holder.
Bingo Different assortments of the key words of a unit are produced on 'bingo' cards. The caller reads a definition and the students can tick the word off if they have the appropriate word on their card (see Template 45).
Splat Divide the class into two teams. Write 10 key words from the unit on the board and provide each team's representative with a swatter. The teacher reads a definition out. The first representative to splat the appropriate word gains a point for their team (see Template 45).
Crosswords Students have to solve and make crosswords based around the key vocabulary of the unit.
Matching/grouping words A vast range of word games can be devised involving grouping or matching the key words of units including naming/identifying shapes or equipment.

☐ **Discussion grids** Use the comparison grid format to encourage students in pairs to discuss the vocabulary/concepts relating to a range of aspects of two things that are being compared. Students can begin this process in pairs; this can then become a whole-class activity with teacher input. The final selection can then become the vocabulary wall poster for that unit of work (see Template 35).

☐ **Role play** Getting students to play the role of key protagonists in whatever your lesson topic may be is an excellent way of getting students to internalise the information, and possibly the processes, that underlie the lesson or unit of work. For example:
– presenting eyewitness account of events;
– public enquiries into issues where groups of students have to present different viewpoints;
– interviews with key protagonists;
– pretending to be the teacher of the topic.
Speaking frames may be needed to help students move into the appropriate register for the roles.

☐ **Speaking frames** Speaking frames can provide students with the suitable opening words of each section of more challenging speaking activities, as well as outlining the content that could be included. They help them build confidence in speaking in a range of registers and in selecting the appropriate register (see Template 72).

☐ **Mime** Any practical activity, incident or play scene can be mimed – this will strengthen students' understanding of the chronology of events or processes and the consequences of actions. A running commentary can be added to this. If you have never considered mime, it is worth investigating. It is a very powerful tool.

☐ **Precise instructions** One student gives the instructions and another follows the instructions. The rest of the class checks that the instructions are being followed correctly, e.g. spoken instructions are given by one student about how to draw a grid for noughts and crosses while another student follows the instructions on the board. Initially the teacher will probably have to be the person who interprets the instructions, as there is a tendency for the student to draw the diagram or do the actions that they know are right rather than listen to the instructions and follow them to the letter.

The following are quotations from 11-year-olds' Science SATs.

■ 'Water is composed of two gins, oxygin and hydrogin. Oxygin is pure gin and hydrogin is gin and water.'

■ 'When you breathe, you inspire. When you do not breathe you expire.'

■ 'H_2O is hot water, and CO_2 is cold water.'

■ 'Germinate: to become a German.'

■ 'Dew is formed on leaves when the sun shines down on them and makes them perspire.'

■ 'Three kinds of blood vessels are arteries, veins and caterpillars.'

The language of learning

The more students can explain the thinking processes that underlie what they are trying to do, the greater will be their understanding both of the tasks in which they are engaged and of the language and vocabulary of the subject. Modelling the thinking process and getting students to talk through what they are trying to do is central to this. The numeracy project is building on this approach.

Joy when the maths adds up

'YES!' Arms punch the air, pupils are jubilant... The triumph among Shirecliffe Junior School's Year 4 was entirely down to getting their maths right.

Pupils were celebrating their quick oral response to the sum of 38 plus 39. They were learning about working with 'near doubles', and Roxanne was at the front explaining the process used to reach her answer – she doubled 30, then doubled eight, added them together and then added one. As she did this, other pupils were waving wildly in the air desperate to respond as well – hence the cheering when the correct figure was revealed.

...During the 40 minutes when pupils learnt about 'near doubles', class teacher Corina Giles constantly required them to explain the process of their calculation, moving them on with praise and encouragement. During the last 10 minutes of the session, pupils seemed keen to show what they had learnt, vying to test their new-found knowledge before the class.

... Corina Giles believes the pace of maths now being taught, and the emphasis on developing mental and oral number skills by discussion, is capturing pupils' attention and achieving real progress: 'Pupils are far more interested in maths now than when they were working through maths schemes individually. They enjoy learning mental strategies; they're not frightened of tackling problems any more'.

(adapted from a TES report, 29 January 1999)

Modelling the thinking process

- I've got to find 17.5% of £36.50.

- Help, that looks nasty.

- What can I remember about percentages? It means out of a hundred, but what good is that to me?

- I remember about 10% – that's ten out of a hundred – but there aren't a hundred of anything here.

- I remember now – ten out of a hundred is the same as one-tenth. Now I can get going.

- 10% of £36.50 is ¹⁄₁₀ of £36.50 – that's £3.65. But how to find 17½%?

- Um ... Ah! As I know 10%, I can find 5% – that will be £1.825.

- And now I'm nearly there because 2.5% is half of 5% – 1.825 divided by 2 is £0.9125.

- Add them all up, and I get £6.3875.

- But what does that mean? £6 and 38.75 pence. There's no such thing as 0.75 of a penny – do I call that 38p or 39p.

- I should round it up since it's above 0.5, so that's £6.39.

- So, 17.5% of £36.50 is £6.39.

Word Bingo/Splat

Maths

parallelogram	rectangle
square	radius
perimeter	triangle
circle	acute angle
obtuse angle	diameter

Music

allegro	adagio
legato	chord
fortissimo	quaver
tenor	crotchet
soprano	semitone

Writing frames

Writing frames (frames that provide the writer with the structure and the opening words of each section of an extended piece of writing) are probably the most useful idea that has been developed in recent years for helping teachers of all subjects to assist students in structuring the order and style of their written work effectively and appropriately. Literacy co-ordinators need to consider whether teachers in all subject areas are thinking about structure as well as content when setting written work. Staff should accordingly be provided with training in the use of writing frames.

Many teachers over the years have come up with approaches that are very similar, but the writing frames referred to here are those developed in Australia and taken up in the UK by David Wray and Maureen Lewis as part of the Exeter Extending Literacy project, EXEL. The Australian genre theorists identified six different types of non-fiction writing, which they termed genres in accordance with the Australian meaning of this word. In the UK genre is normally used to refer to categories of artistic work. This Australian use of genre was adopted by the National Literacy Project, but the framework for teaching for the literacy hour has changed this to 'category of writing'.

Resources

Wray and Lewis's publications are an invaluable way of introducing writing frames to all curriculum areas – *EXEL Writing Frames* and *Writing Across the Curriculum* (both Reading University, see Appendix 7, page 141).

Presenter's notes

If staff are not familiar with writing frames, a practical way of encouraging them to consider why writing frames help is to present them with the task on Template 46, page 82.

Discuss why this is an unreasonable writing task to set. It is unreasonable mainly because, unless teachers have had training in feature writing, they would need some sort of structure to help them, like the feature structure frame on Template 47, page 83.

Most teachers will have read thousands of newspaper articles and features, but very few will have ever written any. Anyone who commissions articles from literacy professionals who are not journalists will discover that most of them will write a report rather than an article, because they are used to writing reports, and automatically fall back into this type of writing. If many literacy professionals need help in structuring their writing into article format, how much more do children need a framework to help them structure new or more advanced types of writing?

Children are too often expected to write independently before they are really ready. In such circumstances most children flounder and the teacher becomes harassed by endless complaints about not knowing how to begin. A writing frame provides the support necessary not only to structure the writing, but also to set the children off in the right direction for each stage of the writing task.

A good introduction to writing frames is the short article by Wray and Lewis that was written for the National Literacy Trust's journal *Literacy Today* (October 1995), and is reprinted here on Templates 48 and 49 (pages 84–85). The article begins by referring to changes in the latest orders for National Curriculum English. The changes referred to are those of 1995 when the article was written. The most recent orders (1999) still reflect this emphasis on the range of non-fiction texts. Quoting from the 1999 orders, *'In KS3, pupils' repertoire in writing and speaking extends to formal and public registers. They develop their ability to evaluate language in use... During KS4, pupils learn to respond with confidence to the language demands of academic study and of the workplace. They use and analyse complex features of language. They read many kinds of texts efficiently and make articulate, perceptive comments on a range of issues.'* There is particular emphasis on non-fiction texts. The following is a useful way of introducing the key points of this article.

☐ Explain to staff that you have organised a trip to a museum and, just as the children are about to get off the coach at the end of the day, you realise that you've forgotten to set any homework. With no preparation, you ask them to write up their trip to the museum and hand it in the following day.

☐ Now ask what these essays, when received, will focus on. (Whether I ask the question in Swansea, Middlesbrough, Birmingham or Hackney the answer is uncannily consistent. Ninety-nine per cent of people answer lunch/food, followed by any arguments that occurred. There is general consensus that the only chance the museum has of a look-in is the shop.)

☐ Model the typical piece of writing that would result, i.e. 'I got up very early on Tuesday because my class was going to... and so... and... and... and then... and then went to bed', well summed up by Wray and Lewis as the 'from bed to bed' style of writing.

☐ Use the recount frame and resultant piece of writing, *A trip to Plymouth Museum* (Template 49, page 85) in OHP form as an example of how a writing frame can transform this sort of writing.

☐ Point out that if teachers are getting 'bed-to-bed' style writing from students, they need to consider how to provide more support to help the students write in a more appropriate style.

Now you are in a position to introduce the six major categories of non-fiction writing. Use Template 50, page 86 to introduce these. They are simply attempts to draw out the key features of the many and varied forms of non-fiction writing, some of which move in and out of a range of genres, so that students feel confident in structuring and expressing their work. Teachers should be aware that students in Year 7 will increasingly be transferring from primary school already aware of the conventions of these six types of non-fiction writing.

Modelling the process

It is important that teachers understand how best to use frames to develop students' writing. Use the Template 51, page 87 (reproduced below) to help staff understand the process.

This oral, teacher-modelling, joint-activity pattern of teaching is pivotal, for it not only models the generic form and teaches the words that signal connections and transitions, but it also provides opportunities for developing children's oral language and their thinking.

It is useful for teachers to make big versions of the frames for use in the teacher-modelling and joint-activity phases. These large frames can be used for the shared writing stage. It is important that the child understands that the frame is a supportive draft and that words may be crossed out or substituted. It is a flexible aid, not a rigid form. Planning should ensure that students have reached the independent activity level prior to beginning any coursework.

Involving children in the process

The greatest potential drawback of writing frames is that children become dependent on them and rely on the teacher to hand out the frame that structures their ideas and sets them off in the right direction. It is essential that development, i.e. systematically increasing the difficulty of the writing that is being tackled, and involving students in the planning process are built into lesson planning.

An example of how to integrate this into unit planning is provided on <u>Template 75, page 117</u>. You may wish to use some of this material here to illustrate the point.

When to use frames

Writing frames should, wherever possible, be located in meaningful experiences rather than used as an isolated study skill. The frame itself is never a purpose for writing. It allows children to rise above the 'and then... and then ...' style of writing. It also helps to prevent them wandering between genre styles. For example, beginning in the third person instructional mode: 'First fry the onion until golden', but then shifting into the familiar recount style with its use of the first person: 'and then I added the tomatoes'.

Be aware that some pieces of writing require the writer to move between different categories of writing; the important thing is to have thought through the appropriate style for each category. An example of a frame for a complex piece of writing is on <u>Template 58, page 94</u>.

Whom to use frames with

Writing frames were originally developed to help students of lower ability, but the very nature of writing frames lends itself to real differentiation. Different frames can be tailor-made for a whole range of abilities. Students with very significant potential can be encouraged by the use of frames to attempt far more complex pieces of writing than they might otherwise do if left to their own devices.

In practice, frames can be useful for students from primary school through to the sixth form, as long as the frames are differentiated to help the student rise to a new level of expression or structure. They are particularly useful for helping to bridge the gap between GCSE and the essay-writing conventions required by many A-Levels. Writing frames can also be adapted by support teachers with SEN or ESL expertise, to create frames that will support the language needs of statemented students or students with specific EAL needs. They are also an excellent device for helping students to build confidence in whatever modern languages they are studying.

Involving students in the process of developing the frames for increasingly complex writing tasks, as suggested in the teaching model, avoids students becoming dependent on the teacher doing the structural thinking for them. Some schools involve older students in discussing with younger ones how frames have helped them tackle specific tasks, for example geography field study.

Writing frames and coursework

The aim for students of all abilities is for them to assimilate the generic structures into their writing repertoires. It is clearly preferable for students not to use frames provided by the teacher for exam coursework since they should then be marked down. A good way forward is for departmental areas to plan their use of writing frames in the years prior to external exams. For example, students in the first two years of secondary school should develop their evaluation and investigation writing skills so that when they are required to write investigations or evaluations for coursework, the appropriate structures are familiar to them. They should quickly outgrow any writing frame.

Familiarising staff with writing frames

A series of handouts is included in this handbook to familiarise teachers with the process:

☐ **The difference between writing frames and question prompt sheets,** see example <u>Templates 52 and 53, pages 88–89</u>. Use <u>Template 52</u> to help teachers get used to the thinking and writing process involved in constructing writing frames. Many teachers have traditionally provided question prompts to help children cope with writing tasks like investigations or evaluations, as in the Year 7 Design and Technology prompt sheet (<u>Template 53, page 89</u>). The key difference between question prompts and writing frames is that writing frames help students begin their responses in the appropriate style, rather than posing questions to be answered. This exercise familiarises staff with this process, though the resultant frame is only suitable for children with limited writing skills.

☐ **Writing generic frames** (<u>Template 54, page 90</u>). The easiest way to get used to devising writing frames is to begin with considering generic frames. *Writing Across the Curriculum* has several examples of generic frames for maths, science and technology departments which could provide a good starting point. Many departments have found that they wish to adapt these frames in the light of experience. To help familiarise staff with this, use <u>Template 54</u> which provides an example of a generic frame for Maths investigations.

☐ **Writing specific frames for specific extended writing tasks** (<u>Template 55, page 91</u>). The specific writing requirements of units of work in areas like humanities and English often do not lend themselves to generic writing frames. Specific frames need to be developed to reflect the structure and content of the piece of writing that is desired. <u>Template 55</u> is a draft frame constructed by an RE teacher, from a school in Birmingham, who had been dissatisfied with the extended writing aspect of a unit of work looking at the rituals of a range of religions.

Use this example to help staff understand how they can adapt frames to suit their purposes. This recount-style frame encourages the students to put themselves in the position of an Orthodox Jewish girl. Point out that an alternative way of handling this is for the teacher to structure the lesson to bring out the differences between the customs of an orthodox Jewish girl on the Sabbath and how students in the class normally spend Friday night and Saturday morning. This could be achieved by amending the comparison planning frame (<u>Template 35 page 65</u>) so that it suited this purpose. A report writing frame could then be constructed to support the writing up of this comparison.

Note: Writing frames have been developed to support non-fiction writing. They should normally not be used to support creative writing because they provide too rigid a framework, which can stultify the student's creativity. There is less of a conventional structure for creative writing than there is for non-fiction text. However, some sort of planning frame appropriate to the creative task in hand is useful. To avoid the blank page syndrome, a possible opening line could be provided to help get children going. There is an example of this approach on <u>Template 68, page 110</u>.

- **Incorporating key words into writing frames** (Template 56, page 92). Key words can be incorporated with writing frames so that students are encouraged to use appropriate terminology, as on Template 56.

- **Moving from a planning grid to a report writing frame to support writing up research** (Template 57, page 93). Planning grids are ideal for focusing work prior to attempting extended non-fiction writing. A unit of work can be planned so that the children begin their research or planning using such an appropriate grid, which will enable them to move more easily to extended writing using an appropriate writing frame, since the groundwork thinking and planning has already been covered.

  Use the report writing frame on Template 57, page 93 to show how a class could have begun their research using the KWL grid on Template 34, page 64 and then written up their research using this frame.

- **How writing frames can raise teacher awareness of the nature of written tasks.** This is explained below, with an illustrative frame on Template 58, page 94.

Some final points

- There is a risk of over-using writing frames. It is all a question of building variety and development into your planning, both for individual teachers, departments and the whole school. Someone needs to have an eye on the overall diet the children are receiving throughout the curriculum in any one term.

- Template 59, page 95 summarises how frames can help students, and offers some advice on how to avoid the dangers.

- The best way to get staff to see the practical benefits of writing frames is to encourage them to start devising writing frames for their area. Section 3 of Template 61, page 98, suggests how to do this within the workshop session. A useful resource for this session is *EXEL Writing Frames* referred to on page 79.

- Template 60, page 96 shows a range of potential approaches to literacy for different curriculum areas using a variety of techniques, including writing frames.

Raising teacher awareness

Writing frames can raise teacher awareness of the nature of written tasks. Attempting to write a specific writing frame for a piece of writing that you have been setting for many years supported by a traditional outline structure, but not by a frame, can be a very humiliating experience. Suddenly you realise just how difficult the piece of writing actually is.

Many teachers, myself included, have realised that they were not really clear about how each section could actually begin. Moreover, the piece of writing you have been setting may turn out to be, on analysis, much more difficult than you had previously recognised. The process of constructing the frame is very instructive, and will be equally so for students when they get involved in the process.

Presenter's notes

An example to illustrate this point is given in Template 58, page 94. It is designed to support a piece of writing on alibis. 'Alibis' is an excellent activity for developing speaking and listening skills, since it involves sophisticated levels of formulating and responding to questions as well as analysing the answers received. The initial idea for alibis came from the 'Sure Fire Lessons'

column of *The Teacher* newspaper many years ago.

- Three members of the class (who are not best friends) are sent outside the class to construct an alibi, pretending that they had been together between the hours of six and nine the previous evening.

- Meanwhile, the rest of the class discusses what questions to ask when they cross-question the alibi group one by one.

The initial group's alibi will be very easy to break, but both the alibi constructors and the cross-questioners learn from the experience and, with each alibi group, it becomes increasingly difficult to break the alibi.

My experience of this unit of work had previously been that the standard of oral work was high, but the written work that I set, analysing the process the students had been involved in, was never at the same level. What my class needed was a writing frame. I had, at one point, considered supporting non-fictional written work with writing frames (I had never heard the term at that stage), but decided, wrongly, that it would be spoon-feeding the students too much.

It was only several years later, having read about writing frames, that I tried to construct one for alibis, and realised just how difficult a piece of writing I had been setting. If you look at the alibis frame on Template 58, page 94 you will see that the frame is a mixture of explanation and report writing (many pieces of writing are an amalgamation of two or more of the categories of non-fiction writing). Moreover, the tense and the person varies depending on the section of the essay being written.

On reflection, it was not surprising that the students' essays had tended to go off in the wrong direction in an inappropriate style.

Homework

Write a 2000-word feature for a Sunday newspaper on how it feels to be inspected by OFSTED/HMI/ESTYN.

Hand it in on Tuesday.

If success is 90% perspiration and 10% inspiration, good feature writing is 10% style and 90% structure. Preparing a clear structure plan is vital to a good feature.

(from Brendan Foley's sidebar to a feature about feature writing, published in *Communicators in Business*, Jan./Mar. 1997)

Beginning

- Introduction that hooks reader into the story. (It need not say what the story is about.)

- A key paragraph that states what the feature is about.

Middle

This contains the bulk of the story, plus any background or back plot. It should also contain quotations that reveal emotion or character. This middle section can be structured with a beginning, middle and end of its own.

Signposts

Changes in the story line from one major paragraph to the next can be marked with a signpost paragraph that points the reader in the new direction.

End

This should include some form of crystallisation of the feature's argument and may include a back-link, or echo, or an idea or image from earlier in the story.

EXEL writing frames

Writing the facts

Written by David Wray and Maureen Lewis, this article first appeared in Literacy Today *in October 1995.*

One of the most interesting changes apparent in the latest orders for National Curriculum English is the way that 'range' now takes pride of place in the various Programmes of Study. Children are to be expected to gain experience of reading and writing a range of texts. Both primary and secondary English teachers would claim they already provide such variety in terms of fiction texts. Certainly, one of the major features of modern approaches to teaching children to read is the emphasis upon broadening children's reading experiences. Yet there remain some problems with non-fiction texts. How can we make sure that the children learn to read and write a range of non-fiction texts? Many teachers will recognise that one of the problems when children work with information texts is that they often do no more than simply copy out passages from reference books with little evidence of learning.

As part of the Exeter Extending Literacy (EXEL) Project based at Exeter University and funded by the Nuffield Foundation, we have been working with groups of teachers to explore ways of broadening and making more effective children's reading and writing of information texts. In this short article we shall outline a way of thinking about the issue of range in factual texts and describe an approach to teaching which seems successful.

Part of the reason for the copying phenomenon referred to earlier is that children lack experience of the different genres of non-fiction texts and their organisational structures. They need some help in distinguishing between these genres in terms of linguistic features such as vocabulary, connectives and structure. In order to provide this help, teachers themselves first need some understanding of these features.

The idea of genre

A concept with a good deal of teaching potential is that of text genre. According to genre theory, pieces of writing which share a common purpose will tend to share a common structure. One language purpose might be to provide instructions for someone else to carry out a task, as, for instance, in a recipe. Such instructions, be they spoken or written, will tend to follow the pattern:

☐ a statement of the goal (e.g. This is how to make a chocolate cake.)
☐ a list of materials necessary to achieve this (e.g. You will need...)
☐ a series of steps to carry out (e.g. First you... then...)

Language patterns such as this tend to become so routine that we are barely aware of them, yet clearly they have to be learnt. Many children will find such structures difficult because they do not have the right expectations about texts. It is quite common, for example, for children to write instructions in the form of a narrative: 'I got some sugar and put it in a mixing bowl. Then I...'. This suggests that teachers need to teach children to use a range of appropriate language structures for appropriate purposes.

In order to do this we need to be aware of the kinds of text genres there are. According to genre theory, there are six: Recount, Report, Discussion, Persuasion, Explanation, Procedural. Research suggests that primary children get a great deal of experience of writing recounts but rarely experience the other genres. This imbalance is important because in later school life and in adulthood these other genres are very heavily used and are crucial to success. Secondary school examinations, for example, demand the ability to write cogent arguments and discussions and if children have not been taught how to structure these forms of writing they will be disadvantaged.

Supporting writing in a range of genres

As a way of introducing children to different written genres and then supporting them in their use of the appropriate text structures, we have found writing frames to be extremely useful. A writing frame provides a skeleton outline for a piece of writing around which children have to structure their own ideas. This outline provides a coherent structure for their writing and scaffolds a range of connectives for them. There are many possible frames for each genre and we have space here for only two examples.

EXEL writing frames

Although I already knew that ....

I have learnt some new facts. I learnt that ....

I also learnt that ....

Another fact I learnt ....

However the most interesting thing I learnt ....

Figure 1

A trip to Plymouth Musem

Although I already knew that they buried their dead in mummy cases I was surprised that the paint stayed on for all these years.

I have learnt some new facts. I learnt that the river Nile had a god called Hapi. He was in charge of the river Nile and he brought the floods.

I also learnt that some times people carried a little charm so if you tell a lie and you rubed the chimes tummy it would be ok again.

Another fact I learnt was they put pretened Scarab Beetels on there hire for decoration

However the most interesting thing I learnd was they mummyified cats and some times mice as well

Figure 2

There is a lot of discussion about whether ....

The people who agree with this idea, such as .... claim that ....

They also argue that ....

A further point they make is ....

However there are also strong arguments against this point of view..

........................believe that ....

Another argument is..

Furthermore..

After looking at the different points of view and the evidence for them I think ....

Because ....

Figure 3

Recount genre

Using the recount frame given in Figure 1, nine-year-old Rachel wrote about her trip to Plymouth Museum (Figure 2). The frame helped structure her writing and allowed her to make her own sense of what she had seen. It encouraged her to reflect upon her learning.

Discussion genre

Using the discussion frame given in Figure 3 helped eleven-year-old Kerry write a thoughtful discussion about boxing (Figure 4). The frame encouraged her to structure the discussion to look at both sides of the argument.

It is vitally important that these frames are not seen simply as worksheets for children to complete. They are only useful when there is a clear purpose for a particular piece of writing. We would also recommend that children need a great deal of experience of other ways of producing writing at the same time as using the frames. Experience has shown, however, that using frames such as these can improve children's writing in a range of genres. They are particularly beneficial for children who find writing difficult.

Boxing

There is a lot of discussion about whether Boxing should be banned. The people who agree with this Idea, such as Sarah.C. claim that if they do carry on boxing they should wear something to protect their head.

They also argue that the people who do boxing could have brain damage and get seriously hurt.

A further point they make is most of the people that have died did have families.

However there are also strong arguements against this point of view. Another group of people believe that boxing should'nt be banned. They say that why did they invent it if it is a dangerous sport.

They say that Boxing is a good sport people enjoy it.

A further more reason is if they ban boxing it will ruin there careers.

After looking at all the different points of veiw and the evidence for them I think boxing should be banned Because five hundred people have died in History Boxing since 1884.

Figure 4

(from *Literacy Today*, October 1995.)

Defining the six key non-fiction writing structures

The following definitions of the six generic non-fiction structures are adapted from *EXEL Writing Frames*, University of Reading.

1 Recount

Purpose To retell events with the intention of informing/entertaining the audience.

Structure usually consists of:
- ☐ a scene-setting opening
- ☐ a recount of events as they occurred
- ☐ a closing statement.

Language features usually consist of:
- ☐ past tense
- ☐ chronological order
- ☐ doing/action clauses.

2 Report

Purpose To describe the way things are; reports can describe a range of natural, cultural or social phenomena.

Structure usually consists of:
- ☐ an opening, general classification
- ☐ a more technical classification (optional)
- ☐ a description of phenomena, often including qualities, uses, parts and function.

Language features usually consist of:
- ☐ present tense
- ☐ non-chronological
- ☐ focusing on groups of things (generic participants).

3 Procedure

Purpose To describe how something is done through a series of sequenced steps.

Structure usually consists of:
- ☐ a statement of what is to be achieved
- ☐ a list of materials/equipment needed to achieve this goal
- ☐ a series of sequenced steps to achieve goal (often diagram/illustration).

Language features usually consist of:
- ☐ simple present tense or imperatives ('do this/that')
- ☐ chronological order
- ☐ focusing on generalised human agents rather than individuals ('first you take' rather than 'first I take')
- ☐ consists mainly of doing/action clauses.

4 Explanation

Purpose To explain the processes involved in natural and social phenomena or to explain how something works.

Structure usually consists of:
- ☐ a general statement to introduce the topic
- ☐ a series of logical steps explaining how or why something occurs. These steps continue until the final state is produced or the explanation is complete.

Language features usually consist of:
- ☐ simple present tense
- ☐ using temporal (then, next, after etc.) and/or causal conjunctions (because, therefore etc.)
- ☐ using mainly action clauses.

5 Persuasion

Purpose Persuasive writing takes many forms, from advertising copy to political pamphlets, but its purpose is to try to promote a particular point of view or argument – unlike a discussion paper which considers alternative points of view.

Structure usually consists of:
- ☐ an opening statement (thesis)
- ☐ the arguments – often in the form of points
- ☐ a summary and restatement of the opening position.

Language features usually consist of:
- ☐ simple present tense
- ☐ focusing mainly on generic human participants
- ☐ using mostly logical rather than temporal conjunctions, therefore not chronological.

6 Discussion

Purpose To present arguments and information from differing viewpoints.

Structure usually consists of:
- ☐ a statement of the issue and preview of main arguments
- ☐ arguments for, plus supporting evidence
- ☐ arguments against, plus supporting evidence
- ☐ recommendation given as a summary and conclusion.

Language features usually consist of:
- ☐ simple present tense
- ☐ using generic human (or non-human participants) rather than personal pronouns (except in the conclusion)
- ☐ logical conjunctions (therefore, because etc.).

A model for teaching with writing frames

When introducing writing frames the following model should be used to help students become involved in the process, rather than letting them become too reliant on structure being provided for them.

■ **Teacher models the process**
through explanation/demonstration

↓

■ **Joint activity**
teacher jointly completes writing frame with class

↓

■ **Scaffolded activity**
students individually use frames to support their writing
– these frames can be differentiated to support/stretch
the full range of students in a class

↓

■ **Involving students in the process**
class given task of creating the frames that
will structure the writing

↓

■ **Independent activity**
students can now structure their writing
without the help of the frame

Comparing writing frames with question prompt sheets

Activity

Turn the question prompts (below left) into a writing frame (below right). Choose an everyday familiar object and evaluate it. Question 1 has been done for you.

Evaluation as question prompts	**Evaluation as writing frame**
Description:	**Description:**
1 What is it supposed to do?	This _____ has been designed to _____
2 How does it do this?	It does this by _____
3 What is it made from?	
4 How is it held together?	
5 What does it look and feel like?	
Evaluation:	
6 How well does it work?	
7 Is it easy to use or not? Explain why.	
8 How much does it cost?	
9 Is it good value for money?	

Design and Technology Year 7 Evaluation

Activity
Choose an everyday, familiar object and evaluate it using the frame below.

Object chosen: _____
(Use the space below to draw a picture of the object and label it.)

Task as question prompts	Evaluation as writing frame

Task as question prompts

Description:

■ What is it supposed to do?

■ How does it do it?

■ What is it made from?

■ How is it held together?

■ What does it look and feel like?

Evaluation:

■ How well does it work?

■ Is it easy to use or not? Explain why.

■ How much does it cost?

■ Is it good value for money?

Evaluation as writing frame

Description:

■ This _____ has been designed to _____

■ It does this by _____

■ It is made from _____

■ It is held together by _____

■ It looks like _____

■ It feels _____

Evaluation:

■ This _____ works/doesn't work well because _____

■ It could be improved by _____

■ It would cost _____.

■ It is/isn't good value for money because _____

Writing generic frames

Below is the first draft of a frame developed by members of the Maths department at Malet Lambert School in Hull.

Writing frame for maths investigations	Teacher's notes
Introduction: The purpose of this investigation is to find out _____	Objective
Stage 1: My first step is going to be _____	Experiment Making Drawing
Stage 2: My results are _____	Encourage to tabulate
Stage 3: I have noticed that _____	Initial pattern Recognition (Algebra?)
Stage 4: By using my results, I predict that _____ **Go to conclusion?** **Extended task:** Having completed the first phrase of my investigation, I am now going to_____. (Go through stages 1–4 again as above)	Predict and test
Repeat again if appropriate My different phrase can be explained by _____ **Conclusion:** Overall my conclusion is _____	Link back to all sections (formal proof)

The Orthodox Jewish Sabbath

How my religion makes Friday night and Saturday special.
(Written from Hannah's viewpoint)

I must make sure that on Fridays I'm home by _____

because _____

When I get home, my mum expects me to _____

When everything is ready, before we can start to eat, we always _____

While we are eating, we talk about _____

After the meal, we _____

The next morning, because I am a girl, _____

Meanwhile, my father and brother _____

Incorporating key words

Key words can be incorporated into writing frames so that students are encouraged to use appropriate terminology, as in the writing frame below which is intended to support children writing about a live drama production.

Key words/concepts	Critical account of live drama
	_____ was performed at _____ on _____
role purpose theme subplot	The play was about _____
voice movement gesture accent humour relationship with audience convincing realistic entertaining authentic charismatic	The most important characters were _____ I thought the best actor was _____ because _____
	Other actors were _____ because _____
freeze frame mime flash back monologue lighting props sound atmosphere	Some techniques they used were _____
design stage	The set was _____
	The best part of the production was _____

A report writing frame

Report frame to support writing up research

I decided to research _____ because _____

I already knew that _____

The three aspects of _____ that I wanted to find out more about

were _____

I discovered that _____

The most interesting thing I found out is _____

I got this information from _____

Alibis

OHP

Activity
Explain the purpose of the game alibis. Using one group's attempt to construct a watertight alibi, explain what evidence there was to support the class's final judgement and what the class learnt from playing alibis.

	Teacher's notes
■ The purpose of the game Alibis is _____	Explanation writing
■ To begin the game, the alibi group (the accused) goes outside the classroom and _____	3rd person present
■ During this time, the rest of the class (the prosecution) discuss _____	
■ It is an entertaining game to play because _____	
■ The group that I have selected to illustrate the game is _____ because _____	1st person present
■ Through interviewing the first of the accused, the prosecution established that _____	Report writing
■ Possible weaknesses to follow up with the next witnesses were _____	3rd person past
■ By the end of the cross-examination the alibi had been _____	
■ The key evidence to support this decision was as follows:	
■ first _____	
■ secondly _____	
■ thirdly _____	
■ finally _____	
■ By the end of this case the class had learnt that in order to construct a successful alibi it is necessary to _____	3rd person past and present
■ The class had also learnt that a successful prosecution should _____	

Benefits of writing frames

The following benefits and dangers of using writing frames have been borne out by discussions with teachers across the curriculum throughout the UK in the many schools and conferences where training has been provided.

Writing frames can help students by:

☐ Curing the 'I don't know how to start' syndrome that often results when students are confronted with a blank sheet of paper.

☐ Providing students with a sense of what they are writing. Writing frames offer a structure and overview for the piece of writing along with the appropriate pronouns (I, you, he, she it etc.) and joining words and phrases (connectives) that form the links within the text.

☐ Reducing the 'and then' style of writing by giving students a range of appropriate sentence beginnings and related connectives.

☐ Raising motivation and esteem by helping students write successfully.

☐ Helping students understand the appropriate structure and style of a range of different types of non-fiction writing.

☐ Discouraging copying by providing a structure that helps students to understand select and structure information appropriately.

☐ Encouraging students to move to higher levels of structuring and expressing their ideas (e.g. bridging gap between GCSE and A-Level or A-Level and degree). If planned appropriately, writing frames are an excellent way of differentiating tasks to meet the needs of all students.

Beware of the following dangers:

☐ Limiting creativity. Writing frames were developed to support non-fiction writing, not creative writing. Students do not have to stick to the frame.

☐ Students becoming too dependent on frames. Avoid this by planning units that include the students in constructing their own writing frames and help them internalise the process so that no frame is needed.

☐ Setting the frames in stone (by printing off hundreds or laminating them for all time). Allow scope for adaptation and development.

☐ Death by a thousand writing frames. There is a danger of over-using writing frames – it is a question of building development and variety into your planning, and monitoring the students' overall diet of writing frames.

Grid to show potential range of approaches to literacy for different curriculum areas

Key:
~ = KS4 only
* = useful
** = very useful

Curriculum area	**Language: speaking and listening**										**Text/writing:**													**Writing frames — generic frames**		**customised frames**
	reviewing lessons	modelling thinking	word games	discussion grids	role play	mime/commentary	relevance game	instructions game	flash cards	speaking frames	sequencing	cloze	prediction	sections	transformation	summary	annotations	flowcharts/diagrams	interrogation	KWL grids	planning frames	thinking frames	jigsaws	evaluation	investigation	frames and key vocab
PSE	**	**	**	**	*	*	*		*	**	*	*		*	*			*		*	*	*	**			** *
Soc	**	**	**	**	*	*	*	*	*	**	**	*	*	*	*	*	*	*	*	**	**	**	**	*		** *
D&T/GNVQ	**	**	**	*	*		*	*	*	*	**	*	**	*	*	*	**		*	*	*	*		** **		* *
Bus/GNVQ	~	~	~	~	~		~		~		~	~		~		~	~	~		~	~	~	~	~		~ ~ ~
IT	**	**	**	*	*			*	*	*	**	*		*		*	*	**		*	*	*	*	**		** ** *
RE	**	**	**	**	**	*	**		*	**	**	*	*	*	*	*	*	*	*	**	*	*	*	*		** ** *
Hist	**	**	**	**	*		**		*	**	**	*	*	*	*	*	*	*	*	**	*	*	*	*		** ** *
Geog	**	**	**	**	*		**		*	*	*	*	*	*	*	*	*	*	*	**	*	**	*	*		** ** *
PE	**	**	**	*	*	*		*	*	*	~	~		~	~	~		~	~	~	~			~		~ ~
Music	**	**	**	**					**	*	*			~	*			**		*	~			~		~ ~
Art	**	**	**					*	*		~		~			*		**	*	*	*			~		~ ~
Dr	**	**	**	*	**	**		*	*	**	*		~	*		*				**	**			~		~ ~
ML	**	**	**	*	*			**	**		*	*		*		*				~				*		** **
Math	**	**	**	*	*		*	*	*				*			*		*		*				**	**	
Eng	**	**	**	*	*	**	*	*	*	**	**	*	*	*	*	*	*	*	**	*	**	*	*	*	*	* * *
Sci	**	**	**	*	*		*	*	*	*	**	**	*	**	*	*	*	**	*	*	*	**	*	**	**	*

Practical workshop and plenary (2 hours)

Adapting existing units of work

 Presenter's notes

Materials needed for this session:

☐ Existing unit of work to be brought by each department

☐ Use Template 61, page 98 for reference, and the handout on page 99 (Template 62) as a guide.

☐ 'What works with boys' checklist (Template 7, page 21)

The purpose of the morning session is to build up to a point where departments can work constructively on adapting existing units of work in the light of the strategies suggested. Every department/curriculum area should bring an existing unit of work to the afternoon session for this purpose.

Have clear learning objectives

To introduce the workshop session, remind staff that they cannot plan effectively without clear learning objectives, both for the whole unit and the specific lessons within it. Point out that the structure of the literacy hour is, in effect, a template or teaching frame to help increase the focus and pace of lessons – a national INSET device. Ask them to consider if there are aspects of it that could help give focus and pace to their lessons. You may wish to remind them of the salient features of the hour at this point.

Checklist of key features of the literacy hour

• A clear statement of the objective of the lesson at the beginning

• A text exemplar of this objective, presented on an OHP, preferably using a white board as screen to maximise flexibility with text (for some areas this exemplar could be an image or object)

• Modelling the objective for the class

• Shared activity/discussion so that the class becomes involved in the process

• Independent or group activity related to the objective – possibly supported by a frame

• Plenary session where the class feeds back on the activity in the light of the objective.

The ultimate planning touchstone should be the learning objective of the lesson, which begins and ends the lesson and guides the teacher in determining what processes to include within the lesson in order to best deliver that objective.

Select the processes to deliver the objective

Ask staff to look at the unit planning grid on Template 61, page 98. It is a useful device for considering the literacy aspect of any unit of work and should help focus on what areas of any existing unit need developing and which processes to select to best do this. To use this grid staff should:

☐ Remind themselves of the key learning objectives of their chosen unit

☐ Highlight the areas they want to focus on, and consider all the questions related to that area and the suggested processes that accompany them

☐ Highlight any questions or processes they think need integrating into their unit planning.

Departments should now be in a position to decide how they wish to adapt their unit of work in the light of these considerations. The What works with boys list (Template 7, page 21) may also be a useful checklist here, to see if all the effective ingredients listed are present within the planning of the unit.

Stress that curriculum areas that do not require significant writing or reading from students should focus on Section 1: Use of language, and consider their unit in the light of this. Remind staff not to import literacy activities, but rather to focus on areas that are integral to the subject they teach. For example, lower school PE gets very little curriculum time, so the focus should be on the language and internalising the processes of sporting activities, not on inventing writing tasks like writing to sports people.

Note that workshops where all curriculum areas only concentrate on this section can be very successful. Such a focus has the advantage of involving all areas in similar discussions so that the feedback is relevant to all. Subject areas that require significant amounts of writing may wish to consider Section 3: Writing, and focus on developing writing frames. Template 60 on page 96 indicates what literacy-related processes have proved successful with specific curriculum areas. This grid will need adapting in the light of the professional experience of teachers within the different areas, but is a useful checklist to help guide departments towards processes they may find useful.

You may also wish to use Template 62, page 99. This is organised along the same lines as the unit planning grid (Template 61, page 98) and includes specific activities in the two middle columns to help departments focus on the literacy aspects of units.

Where to site the session

It is often more effective if this session takes place in the area where the morning session took place. This minimises time lost reassembling for the plenary session and enables the person leading the INSET to join in departmental discussions.

It is advisable for staff to work in groups of two or three once the overall focus of specific curriculum areas has been decided upon. This leads to a far more productive afternoon. Members of the SEN department and EAL teachers may wish to work together or to work with departments that they often support.

The plenary session

A 30-minute plenary session to round off the day provides each area with the opportunity to report back briefly on what they have found useful and what work they are attempting to develop. It gives the literacy co-ordinator a good picture of how staff feel, including which areas may be resisting change.

Reporting back

Each group needs to know in advance that there will be the need for a brief summary of the most important outcomes of the afternoon session for each area. Avoid handing out sugar paper to allow people to present their work visually – this can divert from the real task of focusing on adapting the unit as people start worrying about having a wonderfully designed piece of sugar paper to impress colleagues and tends to make feedback. It is relatively easy for the literacy co-ordinator or some other person to jot down the key points from each group. Obviously this workshop is only the beginning of the process. How to build on this is suggested in the next section (pages 100–118).

Unit planning grid

To be used for checking the extent and variety of literacy processes for any unit of work. Use highlighter pens to indicate which elements are included in any unit (some units will only involve Section 1) and which questions need further consideration.

Title of unit _____ Learning objective _____

Literacy aspect	Questions to consider	Possible approaches
Section 1: Use of language ☐ Vocabulary ☐ Speaking and listening ☐ Language ☐ Discussion ☐ Concepts ☐ Thinking processes	How are the key learning objectives and any thinking processes involved to be modelled?	☐ include in introduction to lesson ☐ other (specify)
	How are pupils encouraged to internalise these processes?	☐ involve class in talking through processes ☐ role-play, mime ☐ reviewing lesson ☐ other (specify)
	How is the vocabulary to be introduced?	☐ discussion grids ☐ explained in context ☐ other (specify)
	How is language consolidated in context?	☐ word games, e.g. dominoes, twenty questions ☐ precise instructions ☐ other (specify)
	How are students helped to use the appropriate register?	☐ speaking frames ☐ other (specify)
	How is language presented to meet the needs of SEN/gifted/EAL students?	☐ differential language tasks ☐ other (specify)
Section 2: Use of text	How are students helped to consider the structure of the text?	☐ sequencing ☐ prediction ☐ sections ☐ flow charts ☐ interrogation ☐ other (specify)
	How are the students helped to understand/select relevant information from the text?	☐ cloze ☐ relevance game ☐ summary ☐ annotating ☐ interrogation ☐ KWL grids ☐ other (specify)
	How are students helped to confront the complexity of a text, or 'the big picture'?	☐ comparison grids ☐ thinking grids ☐ jigsaws ☐ other (specify)
	How is text selected/presented to meet the needs of SEN/gifted/EAL students?	☐ use of pictures to support text ☐ differentiated range of text ☐ other (specify)
	How are students helped to structure their writing?	☐ writing frames ☐ other (specify)
Section 3: Writing	How are students encouraged to structure sentences appropriately, to read work through and to check spelling and punctuation?	☐ relate to exemplar text ☐ apply consistent approach through marking policy and follow up ☐ build into review session ☐ other (specify)
	How are students involved in planning how to structure their writing?	☐ students construct planning/writing frames ☐ other (specify)
	How are students helped to use the appropriate person, tense, etc.?	☐ customised writing frames ☐ other (specify) ☐ oral transformation of person/tense
	How are writing tasks presented to meet the needs of SEN/gifted/EAL students?	☐ differentiated/use of pictures/vocabulary lists/suggested beginning/frames that stretch students ☐ other (specify)
	How are students encouraged to redraft work/use a word processor?	☐ build into unit ☐ teach/reinforce cut and paste skills ☐ other (specify)
	What feedback do students receive and how are they encouraged to evaluate their learning?	☐ periodical review ☐ reflecting on strategies ☐ built into marking system ☐ other (specify)

Workshop – initial tasks for curriculum areas

Unit of work _____ **Learning objective** _____

Activity

Select which aspect below you are going to focus on. Be prepared for someone from your area to report back briefly at the end of the session.

Aspect focused on	Initial planning tasks	Related key tasks	Ideas to consider
1 Vocabulary, discussion and talking through the thinking process used in the unit	☐ List key vocabulary. ☐ List key processes that need to be understood.	☐ Devise tasks to make students aware of the vocabulary and processes focused on. ☐ Devise tasks to raise students' confidence in using this vocabulary and explaining the processes involved.	☐ Look at the ideas on <u>Template 41</u>. ☐ Word walls ☐ Word games, dominoes, etc. ☐ Relevance game ☐ Discussion grids ☐ Mime and commentary ☐ Talking through the process ☐ Reviewing the lesson ☐ Speaking frames
2 Reading, note-taking and research Accessing the texts	List the texts used in the unit	☐ Look at the range of Directed Activities Related to Texts (<u>Template 30</u>). ☐ List the approaches to be used in the unit to help students access the text.	☐ Look at the suggestions on the DARTs sheet (<u>Template 29</u>). ☐ What grids would support the learning process?
3 Significant pieces of writing Understanding the structure of sentences and texts	List significant writing requirements of the unit	What exemplar text will you use? Draft the writing frame to support the significant pieces of writing. Is your frame specific or generic? (Consider using planning frames to structure work leading up to the writing stage.) If you have never written a writing frame, begin by trying to write the frame for a writing task you often set.	Consider which text convention you are using: ☐ Recount ☐ Report ☐ Procedure ☐ Explanation ☐ Persuasion ☐ Discussion (use only a possible opening line for narratives)

Embedding your whole-school approach

Every school will be at a different stage of developing a whole-school approach to literacy and, as stated earlier, one day's in-service training can only provide a start to developing an effective policy. All aspects covered by the training will need to be developed. It is interesting to note that the approach advocated in this handbook seems to match the Michael Fallan model (the Canadian researcher who is evaluating the NLS). He proposes ongoing training to maintain commitment on the grounds that behaviour changes before belief – surface action can change quickly, but deep-seated change takes much longer.

This section suggests ways of developing the following aspects so that real change, rather than surface change, is achieved:
- [ ] Providing time for the development of good classroom practice
- [ ] Building on the literacy hour: developing a whole-school approach to grammar
- [ ] Building on the literacy hour: developing a whole-school approach to non-fiction writing
- [ ] Developing a whole-school approach to marking
- [ ] Embedding literacy in curriculum planning
- [ ] Embedding literacy in development planning.

Providing time for the development of good classroom practice

Departments find training time spent on developing their units of work to maximise their effectiveness most rewarding. Teachers welcome being given the time to reflect on their planning and teaching. It is important that future meeting/training time is found to develop this process and to allow the exchange of ideas.

A future training session could focus on a few curriculum areas. They could provide feedback on which of the ideas developed since the initial training day have worked best. Staff from one area could present their development of oracy within their lessons, particularly concentrating on students explaining the learning processes; another could focus on how they have developed DARTs within their lessons, and a third could demonstrate their use of writing frames. Many teachers shy away from involving students in spoken activities, like discussion and role-play, for fear of the additional control problems that such activities can bring. But every school will have staff who are excellent at handling these processes. Arranging for a department like drama to model a range of techniques for controlling and developing oral group activities is highly recommended. The tricks of the trade may not seem so special to staff in the drama department, but many teachers lack confidence in this area and would welcome the opportunity to widen their teaching repertoire.

The majority of the day could then be used for workshops (preferably in the main hall or similar large area) to allow departments time to continue developing their ideas, with a plenary session at the end to pull the day together. The time to reflect on and share expertise is invaluable. Often staff are vaguely aware of the good ideas their colleagues have, but it takes days like these to pull that good practice together and make it a powerful tool for raising the quality of teaching.

According to Gina Merrett, Headteacher, Norden High School, Rishton, Blackburn, teachers teaching each other leads to improved quality of both the teaching and learning experiences. Her school is taking part in the Key Stage 3 literacy pilot in Lancashire.

Ideally, such a training programme should be linked to a programme encouraging and enabling teachers to see other teachers teaching, both within their own areas and beyond. Heads of areas also need to monitor how the development of the units is working in practice, in the classrooms, so that problems can be rectified and excellent practice identified. Teachers can then be enabled to see examples of such practice. We all tend to get stuck in ruts. Such an approach revitalises teaching; enthusiasm is perhaps the most important ingredient of making learning memorable. (See <u>Template 2, page 13</u> for a draft timetable for this approach.)

Timetabling a schedule of monitoring and observation

Any programme of monitoring and observation requires timetabling to facilitate it. One practical solution is to allow key heads of areas one additional period of non-teaching time per week to be rotated around all their non-teaching time to maximise flexibility. This period can then be used to monitor lessons within their area and to schedule a programme whereby they cover a member of staff, who is then able to observe another member of staff teach, not necessarily within their curriculum area.

Building on the literacy hour: grammar

As explained on <u>pages 40–41</u>, grammar may be very new territory for teachers in many secondary schools. A working group, possibly consisting of the literacy co-ordinator and the heads of English, Modern Languages, Special Needs and EAL should get together and work out proposals for the school's approach to continuing the grammar work begun in primary schools, in particular in the literacy hour.

 Activity
It would be useful to agree the following:

- [ ] **The key terminology to be used**
  This could be selected from the list of terms on <u>Template 19, page 42</u>. How this is to be disseminated to staff, and with what support material, also needs to be planned. The page from the 'Cheshire Cat's Guide to Grammar' (<u>Template 21, page 44</u>) may be a useful resource here.

- [ ] **Training required to make staff feel more confident with these terms**
  Remember that you cannot include something within your teaching repertoire if you do not feel confident about it. Schools may wish to use some of the excellent training material on grammar contained in the primary NLS training pack, in particular the section called *Module 3 Sentence level work – teacher's notes*.

- [ ] **Who is teaching what aspects of grammar and who is reinforcing it?**
  An effective approach would be for the English and SEN departments to teach and reinforce all the key aspects of English functional grammar. The Modern Languages department would then only have to reinforce such grammar while focusing on teaching those aspects of grammar that are functional for the languages they are teaching, but not for English, for example, the dative for German and gender agreement for French. This would

also help EAL teachers to intervene effectively to help students for whom English is not the mother tongue to grasp the basic structure of English.

◢ Presenter's notes

This group may find it useful to use the list on Template 64, page 106, to help them establish a whole-school approach to grammar. Look at the list and decide whether all the points listed as shoulds and should nots are necessary. Are there any points missing that they feel need adding? Their amended list could then be considered by the literacy working party for discussion with all curriculum areas. It could then become part of the school's literacy policy.

The following may be useful to use with staff, including English teachers, who are sceptical about the relevance of grammar:

'Despite my initial reservations I am convinced that the explicit teaching of literacy is an effective and more efficient way of teaching and learning. I'd forgotten that I was a "sophisticated" reader and writer, hence I'd forgotten the rules that were necessary in order to be fully literate. Naming a noun is not important to me now; however for a young person such labelling is of essence, because they need to understand the rules in order that they become independent and progressive readers, writers and orators. Perhaps the example of the noun is too simplistic. In teaching the rules of reading and writing explicitly, and by not assuming how literate my student is, or censoring the language they need to know, I'm more able to empower that student by allowing them to control how and what they read and write.'

Toni Keetley, Literacy Co-ordinator at Chaucer Community School, part of the Sheffield KS3 literacy project, from an article in the September 1999 issue of *Literacy Today*.

All the other departments should recognise their role in reinforcing the appropriate use of grammar for their subject area. This should be reflected in their unit and lesson planning. This approach can be strengthened by implementing the following proposal.

Building on the literacy hour: non-fiction writing

Developing a unit of work in Year 7 to support non-fiction writing across the curriculum

The outline Year 7 unit on Templates 63–74, pages 105–117) builds on the structure, content, focus and processes underlying the literacy hour. It directly relates to the Year 6 Term 3 syllabus, and helps develop links between all the curriculum areas. It is also based on developing students' independence through involving them in the process of constructing and planning a range of frames, as well as using them.

Secondary schools need to build on the understanding of the range of non-fiction texts that students will increasingly face when they transfer from primary school. One possible way forward is to use the varied range of texts that they will experience in secondary school as a springboard to a unit of work that will revise and reinforce students' knowledge about the structure and style of the six key categories of non-fiction writing. The following draft Year 7 introductory unit consists of a series of English lessons underlining the key elements of the six different categories of non-fiction writing, and involves students in the process of planning as well as using frames to support their writing. A range of DARTs activities is included.

Care must be taken to build on what the students already know. In the early years of the literacy hour there will be a very wide range of knowledge, especially where children are transferring from many primary schools, so exactly where to pitch your unit will need careful consideration and built-in flexibility. In the words of one primary headteacher who has taught the literacy hour for the past year, 'There's nothing like children for getting in the way of your planning'.

If other curriculum areas are made aware of this English unit, the texts covered within it and the processes and terminology used to teach it, they can refer to it and use similar processes and terminology when developing the writing appropriate to their area. If it is built on in a way that extends students' understanding and abilities, this should help students transfer and develop the skills they learnt in primary school to all the varied curriculum areas of secondary school. In this way, the problem of students regressing in the first year of secondary education should be overcome. Templates 65–73 (ages 107–115) provide an overview of this unit, with the lesson plans and teaching materials for the first two lessons being provided in detail.

◢ Presenter's notes

Begin by explaining that the unit outlined on Template 65, page 107, builds on the non-fiction work that the students will have experienced in the last term of primary school. The unit is structured to develop their understanding of the conventions of the six main types on non-fiction text. Point out that the unit should emulate the focused, direct teaching approach of the literacy hour, with its emphasis on modelling and teaching the skills related to a wide range of reading, writing and speaking. Remind staff of the key features of the hour listed earlier in the checklist.

Explain that the text focus will be on non-fiction from a range of key curriculum areas. Significant writing tasks are supported by writing frames, but the students are increasingly involved in the planning process for constructing such frames. Point out that the unit makes sense in its own right but, if referred to and built on in the teaching programme of other curriculum areas, it should strengthen all teachers' ability to raise literacy standards across the school. Specifically, teachers in all curriculum areas would be expected to make the type of writing, its structure and key elements explicit to students. Explain that after all significant writing tasks students would be expected to check their work and comment briefly on how successfully they think they have fulfilled the set task.

Then explain that the literacy hour has provided a powerful model for the teaching of writing by explicitly linking reading to writing. Now present Template 66, page 108 to staff rather as you would to a class. As you do so, start to build up vocabulary on a flip chart to illustrate a word wall. Explain that the first lesson then goes on to focus on formal and informal accounts of an incident that led to an exclusion.

A detailed lesson plan for lesson 1 (Template 67, page 109) and its related handout (Template 68, page 110) has been provided to help the English department understand planning in the format of the literacy hour and how to develop this unit of work. I would not suggest using all the templates related to this unit with the whole staff, but rather focus on the ones I am suggesting.

Now use lesson 2 on Template 69, page 111 as an example of how a lesson should begin with a clear statement of its objective. The lesson plan should support this objective. Explain how lesson 2 begins with looking at a short text as an exemplar of the type of writing the students will be required to do later. Show how the teacher models this writing by giving examples and explaining the process (see Template 70, page 112). Explain that this is followed by shared writing where, supported by a frame (see Template 71, page 113), students contribute ideas and the teacher scribes. This is then followed by a scaffolded writing session where the students' writing is supported by the planning or writing frame they have just seen illustrated. The lesson ends with discussion of the conventions of the piece of writing they have undertaken and consideration of how well they have fulfilled them. Point out teaching the grammar and the technical vocabulary related to text is so important because it provides students with the language to discuss text.

You may wish to use the speaking frame on Template 72, page 114 to provide an example of a speaking frame. Use the suggestion on that page as a guide to how to present it to staff.

Activity

End this section by getting the staff to play dominoes (see Template 73, page 115) in groups of three using the vocabulary from the unit's word wall (see Template 67, page 109). Reiterate that this unit should make sense in its own right, but can be adapted to strengthen all teachers' ability to raise literacy standards within the school. Teachers in all curriculum areas would be expected to make the type of writing, its structure and key elements of style explicit to students.

Resources

The QCA publication *Building Bridges and Achieving Continuity at Key Stages 2/3* is useful. Contact: QCA publications line, 0171 509 5555.

The KS3 Literacy Conferences video contains a useful section from Avondale School on a variant of this approach, in which challenging lessons about non-fiction writing are targeted at the school's intervention group.

Developing a whole-school approach to marking

This is another area that carries a health warning. It is a classic area for causing great disagreement, which fails to be resolved by policy that lives only within the covers of handbooks. Meanwhile, in the classroom, teachers continue marking according to their own best judgement, just as they did before the marking policy was established.

More worrying is the fact that hours of teacher time can be wasted on ineffective marking, which the child only glances at while scanning their work for the only thing that they're interested in – the grade they've been given.

There is a tendency to respond to this by trying to establishing standardised marking symbols, so that every teacher throughout the school is supposed to signify erroneous punctuation or the need for a new paragraph by the same set of symbols in the margin. Even if this were straightforward, how constructive is it to focus on showing the full range of textual errors? It may be more useful to take a long view and consider the overall approach as outlined on Template 74, page 116. It might be best to discuss Template 74 first in the literacy

working group and then present the group's proposals briefly either on an INSET day or at a staff meeting.

This approach seems to work with students of a very wide range of abilities. As with any scheme, sensitivity needs to be used when applying it to students who are struggling with basic literacy. The process suggested encourages students to work more accurately in a focused way in all subjects. It also encourages self-assessment. The critical friend approach could then be introduced, whereby students mark each other's work and learn from this process. The suggested marking framework lends itself well to this adaptation.

The issue of a whole-school approach to marking could, at best, only be introduced on a training day. It would need to be discussed at both departmental and joint curriculum level to decide exactly what whole-school marking policy might be implemented.

A note on spelling

Given the nature of the English language, spelling is a tricky area. I sometimes find myself thinking how useful it would have been if some past politician had had Kemal Atatürk's vision and recognised that if you wish to build a literate nation it is useful to have a phonetic script to base it on. (In 1928 Atatürk changed the written language in Turkey from the traditional Arabic script, which did not reflect the vowel–consonant patterns of Turkish, to one based on the Roman alphabet, with a few added umlauts, cedillas and a dotless i ('ı') to cope with the range of vowel sounds.

Doubtless phonetic conformity would get rid of some of the glorious richness of the English language, with its wealth of dialects and imported words that are reflected in the spelling, but research suggests that there are far fewer dyslexics in countries with strictly phonetic languages. However, in reality, teachers have to cope with English as it is. Hopefully the increased primary focus on phonics and spelling will minimise the problem and spelling standards will rise.

It is worth remembering that many spelling 'mistakes' at secondary level come down to carelessness rather than ignorance. The whole-school approach to marking outlined on Template 74 should help to tackle this problem, but clearly it will be beneficial for schools to have an approach to spelling that helps those who do have specific problems in this area. This is very much part of the focused intervention programme that is being outlined to secondary schools in England as part of the National Literacy Strategy.

As far as cross-curriculum approaches to spelling go, it will probably be useful for all departments to bear spelling in mind when presenting the key vocabulary for each unit. The 'look, cover, say, write and check process' is one that is tried and tested and certainly works for many students. In addition teachers should

- Encourage students to look analytically at words, drawing out useful patterns (for example, if you are dealing with geology, relating its spelling to other 'ologies' is useful)
- Help students remember tricky words by teaching them sayings, e.g. the film title *There's Only One R in Sheriff* .
- Involve students in actively identifying the words they need to learn and show them how to learn them.

Schools may wish to set up spelling-log schemes where children keep their own lists of the words they are having difficulties with. When running such schemes the level of difficulty a child has with spelling should be borne in mind, so that children only take on a manageable amount of learning. Those with significant problems should not be further demoralised by the systems set up supposedly to help them.

Focused spelling programmes that students attend, perhaps outside lesson times, have proved successful in many schools.

Embedding literacy in curriculum planning

This is another area with a health warning. It would be very easy to demand that literacy targets and strategies be included in all schemes of work and to set up a system of deadlines and checks to ensure that, on paper, your policy is perfect. But it is only a meaningful exercise if considerations of literacy and appropriate processes genuinely underpin the planning and delivery of lessons. Doing this will take time. A good place to begin is with Year 7, with units as outlined on <u>Template 65, page 107</u> helping to ensure that not only is everyone singing from the same hymn sheet, but that progression is built into planning. Planning for progression in literacy across the curriculum from year to year will not only take time, but will also need revision in the light of progress made, especially if the literacy hour does succeed in significantly raising the standards of students transferring from the primary sector. A useful starting point is considering how the National Literacy Strategy defines what is meant by a literate Level 4 student:

Literate Level 4 student checklist

- Read and write with confidence, fluency and understanding
- Be able to orchestrate a full range of cues (phonic, graphic, syntactic, contextual) to monitor their reading and correct their own mistakes
- Understand the sound and spelling system and use this to read and spell accurately
- Have fluent and legible handwriting
- Have an interest in words and their meanings, and a growing vocabulary
- Know, understand and be able to write in a range of genres in fiction and poetry, and understand and be familiar with some of the ways that narratives are structured through basic literacy ideas of setting, character and plot
- Understand, use and be able to read and write a range of non-fiction texts
- Plan, draft, revise and edit their own writing
- Have a suitable technical vocabulary through which to understand and discuss their reading and writing
- Be interested in books, read with enjoyment and evaluate and justify preferences
- Through reading and writing, develop powers of imagination, inventiveness and critical awareness.

However, such levels of achievement cannot be assumed. Schools need to establish whether this description does cover the majority of their Year 7 intake and then decide how best to build on their findings.

Presenters notes

In the light of this, each department needs to consider which aspects of literacy are most appropriate to its area and how these can be developed and enhanced on a year-by-year basis.

Departmental planning grids A practical way of implementing this is provided by the departmental planning grid on <u>Template 75, page 117</u>, which helps each area to consider how it could develop and support a range of literacy features over time. Stress that this grid should be adapted in the light of the needs of each area and the literacy approach of each school. Completed grids would help the literacy co-ordinator map approaches to literacy throughout the school. <u>Template 75</u> begins by asking whether the way the classroom is arranged supports literacy. You may want to ask staff to consider the following at this point.

Classroom literacy checklist

- Do the walls of the room encourage interest in your subject and relate to current learning, including word walls, appropriate labelling, etc.?
- Are dictionaries and thesauruses easily available?
- Is there a range of differentiated reading and reference material related to the subject?
- Is there access to ICT?
- Can all students see the OHP/board easily?

How the room is organised does make a very significant difference, so it is worth spending time and money on getting this right. Think of how many training days you have sat through when you haven't been able to see the OHP, either because of the layout of the room, the quality of the equipment, the size of the type on the OHP slides or the fact that the presenter is standing in the way. Now ask each area to look at the Year 7 column and decide how it needs amending to fit their subject area. You may wish to refer to the 'Literate Level 4 student checklist'. Then ask them to fill out the Year 9 and Year 11 columns, building in progression. (Point out that for reasons of space years 8 and 10 are missing).

Grids to help analyse the literacy content of units of work Another very useful grid to use here is the unit planning grid on <u>Template 61, page 98</u>, used earlier to helps teachers analyse easily the literacy content and processes of any unit of work. If you tick, highlight or write in the third column how you have met the literacy question posed in the central column, this then makes it obvious which areas you have not covered. For example, if you use this grid to test the Year 7 unit outlined on <u>Template 65, page 107</u> you will soon see that all the areas are covered except for 'How are students helped to understand and select relevant information from text?' On reflection, the unit was not adapted to meet this need since it wasn't an objective of the unit, but it makes it clear that research should be the focus, or at least a significant element, within another unit soon. Over time, the grid serves as a useful tool for reflection on planning.

Building planning into your policy

The timescale for expecting literacy to be included within departmental, unit and lesson planning, with appropriate targets and evaluation, is raised in the opening section of this handbook. It is worth repeating how important it is to give staff the time and the guidance to make this an invigorating process rather than a meaningless bureaucratic task. <u>Template 75</u> suggests a timetable of two years for getting literacy integrated into all unit planning across the curriculum. This may need adapting in the light of progress made.

Embedding literacy in development planning

The art of quality development planning is truly tricky. So much time can be allocated to meeting, discussing, planning and rearranging your ideas in columns, that you can lose sight of actually doing what the plan says. However, unless you have a plan that is well structured around who is going to lead what by when in the hope of achieving what, then there is no hope of arriving at your destination. It is therefore vital that literacy, which underpins so much that schools are trying to achieve, is integral to effective school development planning.

The material available to LEAs to distribute to school managers in England at the Key Stage 3 literacy conferences is very useful for this (KS3 Literacy Conferences, LEA file).

Presenters notes

Particularly impressive, if daunting and somewhat oddly ordered, is the unattributed 'Where are we now?' planning frame on pages 74–75 of the above document. For the sake of clarity, it is presented here (Template 63, page 105) with its columns moved round and adapted slightly so that it moves in the direction in which you are trying to go. The descriptors in this grid take you through the various areas that would need to be integrated into the overall school development plan.

Looking at the third row, 'Delivery of learning/teaching processes', the 'Emerging' column in the original document reads:

- The emphasis on the curriculum is content, and the delivery of content is pitched at 'the middle' of the class.
- Students with identified literacy and learning needs are placed in English focus classes.

By the final embedded column this has become:

- The assessment of the literacy demands of texts and tasks set is embedded in the practice of teachers
- All subject departments vary the delivery and adapt the content of courses to address individual student's literacy and learning needs
- School policies acknowledge research that supports intervention in mainstream.

Literacy co-ordinators may find the grid on Template 63 a useful tool for plotting where they are now in relation to the five aspects outlined on the grid, and where they hope to be by particular dates.

The purpose of this handbook has been to give you a practical route to embedding literacy in the planning of all teachers through staff professional development, the second row in the table. In this row the 'Emerging' column in the original document reads (with my alterations in italics):

- ☐ A few teachers have been provided with quality professional development in literacy and learning.
- ☐ Staff, *including management*, have not seen the need to participate in professional development in this area.

By the final 'Embedded' column this has become:

- ☐ Teachers in all subject areas have undergone quality professional development in literacy characterised by:
- ☐ The availability of theory, demonstration, practice, feedback and coaching
- ☐ A climate of peer support
- ☐ Spaced learning
- ☐ A whole-school approach

- ☐ Action research
- ☐ The professional development resulted in teacher reflection and embedding of literacy strategies in the teaching of content
- ☐ Each year, staff undergo on-going quality professional development in literacy and learning.

Where are we going? Planning grid

Aspects to consider	Emerging	Developing	Functional	Embedded
1 Level of whole-school commitment				
2 Staff professional development				
3 Delivery of learning/ teaching processes				
4 Monitoring and evaluating				
5 Students' literacy outcomes				

The role of grammar in a whole-school approach to literacy

Any approach to grammar should:

- Establish the key terminology to be used across the curriculum
- Acknowledge and build on what students already know
- Involve students in exploration and investigation
- Encourage interest in and respect for all forms of language
- Focus on the functions of grammar in real texts
- Address structures and patterns beyond the sentence
- Relate directly to the issue of how language changes in relation to purpose and audience
- Develop awareness of grammar through reflection on the students' own writing in the process of drafting
- Ensure all staff are trained in the school's approach to grammar so that they are able to structure their lessons in a way that will strengthen it.

Any approach to grammar should not:

- Focus predominantly on errors
- Rely on invented sentences out of context
- Forget that function is central.

Year 7 draft unit – The ingredients of different types of writing

Whole-school planning objective : Developing non-fiction writing across the curriculum

Build on students' existing knowledge and help them recognise the conventions of a wide range of non-fiction texts and use them appropriately when reading and writing in all subject areas. Help all staff develop the students' ability to read and write effectively through using shared terminology and approaches across the curriculum.

Part 1: Introduction to unit

Objective: Identify different types of writing and related terminology about structure and style. Compare the structure and language features of a formal and an informal piece of writing on the same incident (see Template 66 for an example).

Part 2: Formal letter reporting on same incident

Objective: Show how the layout, structure, style and tone of a text relates to its purpose. Use a writing frame to assist structure. The plenary session focuses on establishing the typical features of a formal letter (see Template 69 for an example).

Spoken extension to parts 1 and 2

Objective: Encourage students to speak in a range of registers appropriate to differing situations. Build familiarity with the structures of more formal spoken English in preparation for formal writing (see Template 72 for an example).

Part 3: Recount writing: Text

Objective: Build understanding of the conventions of recount writing. Select a piece of recount writing as an exemplar. Students recount orally any recent shared experience, for example a visit to an art gallery. Build on what you have focused on in the previous lessons. Involve class in construction of appropriate writing frame, focusing on logical structure for the task to support writing a formal recount of the visit. The plenary session focuses on establishing the typical features of recount writing.

Part 4: Report writing

Objective: Build understanding of the conventions of report writing. To help underline the importance of structure, select a short historical text that compares and contrasts two things suitable for sequencing. The students sequence the text appropriately. Focus on connectives and tense. Then they construct a comparison grid for the passage they have just sequenced. The plenary session focuses on establishing the typical features of report writing.

Part 5: Procedural writing (instructions)

Objective: Build understanding of the conventions of procedural writing. Look at an exemplar piece of DT text. Focus on imperative and use of second person, plus careful use of pronouns so that instructions are unambiguous. Practise precise use of language by asking students to give clear instructions about how to get from one part of the school to another. Students then write instructions for getting from one part of the school to another. Focus on clarity of instruction, logical order, connectives and use of imperatives. Support with a list of useful phrases. The plenary session focuses on establishing the typical features of procedural writing.

Part 6: Explanation writing

Objective: Build understanding of the conventions of explanation writing. Select a passage explaining a scientific phenomenon. In groups, students divide the text into sections by establishing what distinguishes one section of text from another. They then construct the writing frame that would support that piece of writing. Focus on structure and use of connectives. The plenary session focuses on establishing the typical features of explanation writing.

Part 7: Discursive writing

Objective: Build understanding of the conventions of discursive writing. Select a topic on which there is a range of viewpoints. Use the jigsaw technique to get different groups to focus on one aspect of the subject in order to report back to the whole group. Once each group has reported back, focus on how to structure a range of viewpoints, including your own. The class then constructs appropriate planning and writing frames to support this type of thinking and writing. The plenary session focuses on establishing the typical features of discursive writing.

Part 8: Persuasive writing

Objective: Build understanding of the conventions of persuasive writing. You could use the same topic as for discursive writing, but this time focus on persuading the audience to think/act in a certain way. Include discussion of neutral and emotive language. Involve the class in deciding on an appropriate writing frame, which should then be used. The plenary session focuses on establishing the typical features of persuasive writing.

Concluding session

Objective: Reinforce understanding of the conventions of non-fiction text and related terminology. Look at short extracts from a wide range of texts, as in the opening session, to consolidate the class's understanding of type of text and purpose, related to structure and style. Include word games like dominoes (see Template 72) or bingo to reinforce the vocabulary and concepts of the unit, using words from the word wall (see Template 66).

The ingredients of different types of writing

- ■ **What type of text is it?**
- ■ **What evidence have you to support your answer/**
- ■ **Who is the audience of the text?**
- ■ **What is the purpose of the text?**

---

1 Thinly peel the potatoes and cut them into even-sized pieces. Put them in a saucepan, cover them with boiling water, add some salt, bring to simmering point and cook for 15 minutes.

---

2 Take a little exercise,
Take a healthy diet,
And take Hermesetas.
The sweet, calorie-free alternative to sugar.
Hermesetas helps you take good care of yourself.

---

3 Friendly, outgoing, used to talking to people, computer literate – then why not talk to us about joining our telesales team? An attractive package awaits the successful applicant.

---

4 Forget about affairs of the heart for the moment, even if you find yourself pining today. Still, work comes first, and for that you should be in formidable form...

Introductory unit: The ingredients of different types of writing

Year 7, Lesson 1

Lesson plan

Unit objective
Recognise and use appropriately the conventions of a wide range of non-fiction texts.

Objective of lesson 1
Introduce the specific skills within first lesson's objective, emphasising the final objective as the one that will be focused on in the plenary session:
- ☐ Identify different types of writing and terminology related to structure and style
- ☐ Compare the structure and language features of a formal and an informal piece of writing on the same incident – relate to audience and purpose.

Part 1 (15 minutes) Introduction
Introduce how the course will build on students' existing knowledge of language so that they become confident in recognising and using the conventions of layout, structure and style for a wide range of texts when reading and writing.
Using Template 66, identify different types of text. Read out a piece of text and then ask the class the following questions, allowing short discussion time with partner before anyone answers to maximise participation:
- ☐ What type of text is it?
- ☐ What evidence is there for deciding this?
- ☐ Who is the audience of the text?
- ☐ What is the purpose of the text?

Briefly introduce some of the key features, focusing always on the purpose/audience of the piece of writing and such things as tone, person, tense. All these points will be revisited regularly throughout the unit. Begin building up key vocabulary on your word wall.

Part 2 (15 minutes) Shared reading and role play
Allotment incident as a formal report; allotment incident as an informal autobiographical recount.
Using Template 68 as an exemplar of formal report writing, read and discuss the formal report of the allotment incident. Through discussion, bring out how the tone and structure maximises the 'facts' and chronology of the case while minimising any exciting atmosphere. Stress the use of the third person and impersonal structures like the passive (e.g. *The incident was investigated*) and the formal use of language. Then introduce autobiographical style of recount writing based on the report of the allotment incident. Model for the class how they might pretend they were George and recount the incident from George's point of view. Stress first-person, informal, colloquial-style narrative. Ask members of class to role-play being George and to tell his story as if he were telling his friends what had happened.

Part 3 (20 minutes) Individual writing task
- ☐ Resources: Summary of incident (Template 68)
- ☐ Task: Write George's version of the allotment incident. 'Pretend you're George and write the story from his viewpoint.'

  Fifteen minutes before the end of the lesson, ask the class to read their stories through, checking them carefully and correcting their draft as appropriate, and then ask them to write a brief comment about how well they think they have completed the task.

Part 4 (10 minutes) Review
Ask some students to read out their stories. Afterward the class discusses whether the stories have the appropriate structure and style, then discusses how these accounts differ from the formal report. Students should be encouraged to use vocabulary from the word wall.

Word wall
procedural   instructions   imperative   chronological   second person   autobiographical
style   register   informal   recount   first person   dialect   colloquial   formal   passive

The allotment incident

The following is a factual report of the events leading up to George's three-day exclusion from school.

At breaktime on 9th September 1998, a Year 8 boy called George Price kicked his football into the allotments next to the school playground. He climbed over the fence to retrieve it. (There is a clear notice on the fence telling students not to climb over, and this message is regularly reinforced by staff.)

An old man digging his potatoes on the allotment shouted at George not to tread on his vegetables. George became very rude and started threatening and pushing the man. The man complained to the school.

The incident was investigated.

The head decided to exclude George for three days because such behaviour was typical of the way George had treated people when he was in Year 7, and other methods of punishing him had clearly failed to modify his behaviour.

 Activity – George's version of the allotment incident
Pretend you're George and retell the story from George's viewpoint.

You could begin with this line if you would like to:
'Well, I was Alan Shearer, see. I kicked the ball really hard and it just...'

☐ Next, check your story and alter it to make it both more effective and more technically accurate.

☐ Remember that this is informal writing, so your language and grammar could reflect the informal speech or dialect of the speaker.

☐ Look back at the original report and think about the differences between your piece of writing and the report.

☐ Finally, write a brief comment on how well you think you have completed the task.

Introductory unit: the ingredients of different types of writing

Year 7, Lesson 2

Lesson plan

Objective

To show how the layout, structure, style and tone of a text relates to its purpose.
Example text – formal letter.
Specific skills within the second lesson's objective are:

☐ Layout of formal letter and structure of letter text, including appropriate connectives
☐ Summary
☐ Formal tone, phrases and vocabulary appropriate to the text
☐ Use of first and third persons
☐ Use of tense – how and why it changes within the text.

Part 1 (15 minutes) Introduction to text

Using the OHP of a typical school exclusion letter (Template 70), focus on layout, structure and content. Then focus in detail on the style that relates to this content:

☐ Formal tone, phrases and vocabulary appropriate to the text
☐ Use of the first and third persons
☐ Use of tense and how and why it changes within the text

Part 2 (15 minutes)

Introduce the writing frame for the exclusion letter relating to allotment incident (Template 71). Discuss how the exclusion letter relating to the incident would be structured and what its style would be. Put the frame on the board and model the process. Then involve the class in jointly constructing the letter.

Part 3 (20 minutes) Individual writing task

☐ Resources: exemplar exclusion letter still on OHP (Template 70) – covers useful vocabulary and phrases. The jointly constructed letter is no longer on display.
☐ Task: using the writing frame to support the work, write a three-day exclusion letter to the boy's parents explaining that he is being excluded because of his aggression towards a member of the public.
☐ Fifteen minutes before the end of the lesson, ask the students to read their stories through, check them carefully, correcting their draft as appropriate, then write a brief comment about how well they think they have completed the task.

Part 4 (10 minutes) Review

☐ Ask some students to read out their letters. The class discusses whether the letters have the appropriate structure, style and tone given the letter's purpose. Conclude the lesson by asking the class to decide the key ingredients of a formal letter.

Words for a word wall

The following words should be added to your word wall: layout   present tense   style   tone
summary   third person   tructure   draft

Exemplar exclusion letter

Mr and Mrs Cooper
32, Sheen Court
The High Street
Leyton
London E10 4PJ

**Broadgreen School
Victoria Street
Leyton
London E10 2AH**

9th September, 2000

Dear Mr and Mrs Cooper

I regret to have to inform you that we are excluding Susan from school for three days, from Friday 10th September to Tuesday 14th September inclusive, because she was involved in a very vicious attack on a student from another school.

After school on the last day of the summer term, Tuesday 21st July, a group of girls from Susan's class set off towards Kingsway High School looking for a girl whom they felt had been spreading rumours about them. They found their victim at a bus stop and, having initially taunted her, then proceeded to punch and scratch her. A member of the public fortunately phoned the school. Your daughter has admitted that she took a leading part in this assault.

Clearly such behaviour cannot be tolerated and brings the school into disrepute. We therefore feel that we have no choice but to exclude Susan for three days to try and make her realise the seriousness of her situation. As you are aware, she has been warned before about such behaviour, but does not seem to be taking any notice of the school's and your repeated warnings. I have enclosed a leaflet that outlines your rights relating to exclusion.

Please bring Susan to school at 8.30 a.m. on Wednesday 15th September to see her Head of Year, Mrs Wells, so that we can discuss this very serious situation.

Yours sincerely

J. Bishop, Headteacher

Mr and Mrs Price
28, Sheen Court
The High Street
Leyton
London E10 4PJ

Broadgreen School
Victoria Street
Leyton
London E10 2AH

23rd September, 2000

Dear Mr and Mrs Price

I regret to have to inform you that we are excluding George from school for three days, from Friday 24th September to Tuesday 28th September inclusive, because of . . . .

At breaktime on Tuesday 9th September, George . . . .

I therefore feel that I have no choice but to exclude George because . . . .

As you are aware, George has previously . . . .

I have enclosed a leaflet that outlines your rights relating to exclusion.

Please bring George to school at 8.30 a.m. on Wednesday 16th September to see his Head of Year, Mr Miller, so that we can discuss this very serious situation.

Yours sincerely

J. Bishop

J. Bishop, Headteacher

Speaking frames

Several possible conversations arising from the allotment incident lend themselves to the construction of speaking frames, e.g. a telephone conversation between the head teacher and the allotment holder, or the Head of Year's conversation with and Mr/Mrs Cooper at the end of the exclusion. Below is an example of how the speaking frame for the telephone conversation with the allotment holder could be structured.

Task

Introduce the following situation: In pairs, students are to role play being the head teacher phoning the allotment holder (Mr Brown).

Scenario

The head teacher's aim is to try and reassure the allotment holder that the school has taken his complaint seriously, appropriate action has been taken and that more care will be taken to try to prevent such incidents occurring in future. The key purpose of the call is as a damage limitation exercise to minimise local gossip about how bad the school is. The old man is pleased that the school has bothered to phone him, but very annoyed with all the problems he's had with local students over the years, and is not going to miss an opportunity to tell the head this. He will be speaking in whatever is local informal speech. Each student takes a turn playing both roles, and each pair tries to perfect the conversation ready for presentation in a plenary session.

Speaking frame to support the head teacher's telephone call to Mr Brown, the allotment holder

Be aware that the head teacher will have to adapt her speech to Mr Brown's replies and listen to what he has to say, but she will wish to include all the following areas in the conversation and to win him round as much as possible. Note that the head teacher is using 'we' to stress that she is speaking on behalf of a united institution, though she may choose to say 'I' occasionally to stress personal commitment and reassurance.

Head teacher phoning allotment owner

Areas to cover

Reassure school taking incident seriously – boy to be punished by exclusion.
Allow Mr Brown to tell whole incident again to get it off his chest. Make reassuring comments, then move to second point. This tactic will be used throughout to head off Mr Brown's endless list of grumbles.
Cover the sorts of things the school did to investigate the incident to show the school in a good light.

Explain what steps have been taken in the light of the incident. Include:
- [ ] All students have been made aware of seriousness of incident via assemblies.
- [ ] Boy's mother has been up to school to discuss the situation and wishes to pass on her apology for her son's behaviour – she will be arranging for George to write a letter of apology.
- [ ] School will be approaching governors for funding to improve fencing in hope of preventing balls from being kicked over into the allotments in future.

End with repeat apology and reassurance. Include fact that he shouldn't hesitate to phone if further problems.

Possible introductory statements for each section

Hello, Mr Brown, this is Mrs Bishop from Broadgreen School speaking. I just thought I'd ring to reassure you that ....

We're so pleased that you rang to complain. At Broadgreen School, we always take such complaints most seriously. As soon as you rang, we ....

In the light of this incident we are ....

I am so pleased to have has this opportunity to tell you how ....

Word dominoes

Based on the word wall for the Year 7 unit 'The ingredients of different types of writing'.

chronological	tense		non-fiction	narrative

structure	imperative		passive	explanation

introduction	adjective		impersonal	first person

conclusion	description		persuasion	audience

factual	instructions		discussion	verb

logical order	adverb		subject	noun

recount	formal		connectives	sequence

pronoun	informal		autobiography	report

second person	description		information	opinion

procedural	dialect		colloquial	tone

For any piece of significant writing:

■ Teachers should inform students, when a piece of work is set, what aspects of the work it will be marked for.

■ Students should read their work through carefully and correct errors before handing it in.

■ Students should write a comment on the bottom of their work assessing how well they think they have completed the task set. Work will be returned unmarked if this has not been done.

■ Teachers should make their comments in the light of the student's comment. The purpose of the teacher's comment is to suggest constructive ways forward for the student to improve whatever aspect is the focus of the work. The comment should help to engage students in a dialogue about their work.

■ Close-marking for all errors should usually be limited to the first half-page. The English/SEN marking scheme could be used for this. (This close marking should often consist simply of underlining all the errors within half a page, or stating in the margin the number of spelling, punctuation or expression errors to look out for. The following lesson would then begin with students, in pairs, working out what needs to be corrected to make the passage right.)

■ Marking should be related to the literacy targets of students identified as having difficulties in this area.

Departmental developmental planning guide

Subject area: _____

This grid should be amended to suit the demands of individual curriculum areas. Additional questions to be considered are: Does the way my classroom is arranged support literacy? Does it encourage reading related to subject?

Literacy aspects	Year 7	Year 9 (What skills focused on)	Year 11 (What skills focused on)
☐ Speaking and listening ☐ Thinking skills ☐ Vocabulary	Model talking through the learning processes involved, include reflection on learning through DARTs discussion activities and plenary sessions. Identify subject-specific vocabulary and related contexts for each unit – consider how this is made explicit in lesson plans.		
☐ Reading and accessing text	Model reading of texts. Encourage paired/ group reading. Have a subject-specific book box to encourage students to extend their knowledge and interest. Ensure range of approaches to texts included within each unit to support text interrogation and reflection skills.		
☐ Research skills (Establish where these are being taught.)	Conduct at least one investigation during the year using controlled resources (i.e. not the whole library) and geared so that students practise/develop research skills. Students have access to CD-Roms and Internet for research.		
☐ Writing	Provide appropriate text as exemplar. Model writing skills. Include at least one piece of extended writing per unit, supported by planning/writing frames and involving redrafting on word processor if possible. Appropriate frame templates available and text for editing on screen.		All students now internalised key structure of writing required for GCSE. Introduce advanced planning and writing skills to prepare for A-Levels.
ICT (Establish where ICT skills are being taught)	Integrated into subject.		
Planning Literacy objectives integrated into planning	By January 2000	By September 2000	By September 2001

Conclusion

The benefits of adopting a whole-school approach to literacy along the lines I have been advocating are summed up by Gena Merrett, Headteacher, Norden High School, Blackburn:

'It may be some years before any impact of our literacy strategy upon student outcomes can be identified. However, its effect upon the quality of teaching and resources, upon the confidence and development of staff, and upon the sharing of good practice is much in evidence. This has not only improved the learning experiences of our children, but will lay a firm foundation for future development.

While our literacy strategy is about developing confidence with and mastery of language, it is predominantly about improving teacher recognition of the role and the power of language in the learning process, and improving the quality of teaching and learning. Teachers are the difference between good and bad learning experiences for students. Our literacy strategy is powerful because it invests in the teaching and learning of the whole community.'

(*Literacy Today*, June 1999.)

Her school is part of the Key Stage 3 literacy project in Lancashire. This perspective is reinforced by Stephen Capper, the literacy co-ordinator for Little Ilford School, Newham (which is also a Key Stage 3 literacy pilot school) who said

'A particular strength of the project is the willingness of all teams to take responsibility for literacy development in their area and to see it as a strengthening of their subject and the school rather than a sideline, a distraction or someone else's responsibility... the 'Literacy Umbrella' is exactly about school improvement, school effectiveness and improving the quality of teaching and learning.'

(*The English and Media Magazine*, Summer 1999.)

A school must be a learning organisation for teachers as well as students. Just as the literacy hour provided an in-service training template to help teachers focus on the processes that underpin learning, so secondary schools can learn from and build on that template to strengthen teaching across the curriculum.

As the copy deadline for this handbook raced towards me, I found myself sitting in a theatre staring at a screen on which the words 'From Playdough to Plato' were written. I was miserably thinking that, with so much work to do and so little time, I shouldn't have come away from my computer screen to listen to speakers at the Pre-school Learning Alliance's annual conference. The quality of the morning's presentation soon taught me otherwise. The only page of this book that I felt was seriously in need of rewriting was the conclusion, which was sinking in a mire of pomposity, but fortunately I was inspired by Alan Tucket. At the end of his presentation, but with the heading 'The key skills of adult learning', he put the following on screen.

The vital ingredients of a whole-school approach to literacy

- Dreaming
- Stealing
- Dancing
- Showing off

In the light of Alan Tuckett's second commandment, I felt free to plagiarise and have adapted the slide and his explanation as follows.

Dreaming Being imaginative and thinking beyond tramlines will be essential to the creation of an invigorating approach. Do not get buried in the bureaucracy of policies, but keep thinking lively thoughts. And, most of all, don't lose sight of the dream of every student having so mastered the skills of reading that they can soar through the challenges and delights of a highly literate society.

Stealing There are some wonderful ideas around, both inside each school and in the wider education world and beyond. Share them, develop them, use them. And, most importantly, provide opportunities for staff to share and develop their thinking.

Dancing Someone once said, 'If I can't dance, I don't want to join your revolution'. Creating a whole-school approach to literacy could revolutionise teaching in a school, and it should be fun. Sharing good ideas is a revitalising, interesting, intellectual experience. Maximise the opportunities for reflection and exchange of ideas, and enthusiasm will flow. Teachers need to be enlivened by the process to want to get involved.

Showing off If we do not tell people about what we are doing, they won't know about our ideas and therefore won't be able to use them. We need to learn from each other. The Internet provides a great opportunity to share ideas and feedback on how your school is developing its whole-school approach to literacy. You can e-mail me with comments or share your ideas by adding to the Visitors' Page on the National Literacy Trust's website (www.literacytrust.org.uk). Best of all, use the secondary section of the discussion boards on the website so that it is easy for anyone interested in whole-school approaches to literacy to exchange ideas.

Appendix I Useful HMI checklists

The inspection material below by John Hertrich, HMI, from the HMI survey of literacy in 1997 and the subsequent inspection of the Key Stage 3 literacy projects in 1998, provide useful checklists for your whole-school approach to literacy.

The following lists have been included:

- ☐ The seven major conclusions from the Secondary Literacy survey, 1997
- ☐ Features of successful practice from the above survey
- ☐ Ten critical dimensions arising from the Key Stage 3 projects
- ☐ Thirteen key issues arising from the projects for other schools
- ☐ The Ofsted remit for literacy at Key Stage 3
- ☐ The HMI form for considering literacy

Those that have been boxed are probably the most immediately useful for literacy co-ordinators. Both reports are available in full on the NLT website: www.literacytrust.org.uk/Database/wholeschool.html.

Secondary Literacy, a survey by HMI, Autumn 1997

The seven major conclusions

- ■ Secondary schools are at a comparatively early stage in the development of students' literacy, but successful practice is already evident in some.

- ■ There is no 'quick-fix' solution for deficiencies in literacy.

- ■ Considerable efforts are often put into literacy development, but many schools do not monitor or evaluate the outcomes of their efforts.

- ■ A multi-strategy approach to literacy development is more likely to be successful than the adoption of a single strategy.

- ■ Approaches that involve curriculum areas other than English, together with work done in English departments, are more likely to be successful than initiatives that are confined to English and/or SEN departments.

- ■ There are other 'literacies' besides reading and writing.

- ■ Literacy development is inextricably connected with the development of the whole young person and is linked to students' perception of themselves and their place in the world.

Features of successful practice from the Secondary Literacy survey

Looking across the whole sample, rather than individual schools, the most important features of successful practice are as follows.

- ☐ The school sees literacy as the key to improving learning and raising standards and has an approach which is relevant to all curriculum areas and students of all levels of attainment.

- ☐ There is a clear rationale, understood by staff and governors and shared with parents and often students themselves. Typically, this includes appropriate definitions and ways in which literacy relates to English, 'communication' key skills and 'language', and to other subjects. The crucial role of listening and speaking is spelled out and the model of literacy includes, but goes beyond, adult needs, access and the purely functional.

- ☐ A detailed assessment of students' attainment has been carried out (for example, a scrutiny of Key Stage 2 test results and baseline reading, spelling and comprehension testing in the first term of Year 7). This is used as the basis for longitudinal, coherent and consistent monitoring and evaluation of students' progress.

- ☐ The school identifies priority areas, especially in Key Stage 3, and has introduced one or more specific interventions. Particular attention is given to those students whose reading age is significantly below their chronological age.

- ☐ The school recognises the specific needs of its student population, such as those who are learning English as an additional language or who have special educational needs, takes steps to co-ordinate the contribution of those who have responsibility for these areas, and disseminates information and best practice across all departments.

- ☐ As a result of the points listed above, the school has set targets for improvement that relate to specific groups of students and to individuals. Targets are linked to the school's short-, medium- and long-term planning.

- ☐ Staff have carried out an audit of the literacy needs of various subjects, including types of text being used, reasons for reading and kinds of written response expected from students. The results are made clear to all staff and there are mechanisms to influence teachers' methodology in classrooms.

- ☐ The headteacher and senior management team are fully committed to the literacy initiatives, have a good understanding of what is involved, and are aware of the quality of the school's existing work in this field. Their commitment extends beyond the limits of a short-term project.

- ☐ A management group takes responsibility for the detailed planning of the work and the group has, as part of its remit, the monitoring and evaluation of initiatives, including their impact on students who are involved in more than one initiative. It is not essential to create a new post to co-ordinate the school's literacy work, but the group should include senior and middle managers and represent the interests of the English department, SEN, EAL and aspects and subjects. Literacy development can be equally successful when managed and led by an individual member of staff.

- ☐ Attention is paid to discovering parents' perceptions and priorities and to raising levels of their awareness and involvement.

- ☐ The school's initiatives are underpinned by clear, succinct documentation for all staff, including, policies, development plans and guidelines.

- ☐ There is a core of approaches or interventions which is sustainable and which provides good value for money.

- ☐ Teachers are given the necessary training and have continuing opportunities to discuss progress. Key members of staff are knowledgeable about developments in primary schools, especially approaches to the teaching of reading and writing and the NLP Framework.

- The English department defines its own contribution to the school's literacy work but is not seen as solely responsible.
- The school receives external support from LEA advisers/inspectors, consultants or others, and/or it works closely with other institutions, such as contributory primary schools.
- The school has costed its literacy work and has at least begun to improve its resources. This includes the provision of 'literacy-supportive classrooms'.
- All departments accept a high degree of responsibility for teaching literacy within their own subjects and this is clearly articulated in the school's strategic response to the issue.

Ten critical dimensions arising from the Key Stage 3 projects

From the HMI's inspection of the Key Stage 3 literacy projects, the following ten critical dimensions were identified:

- The management of the project is effective in practice in each school
- A substantial number of staff are actively involved in any literacy development in each school
- The school's approach to literacy development generally is multi-layered as opposed to relying on a single intervention
- The project is institutionalised in each school
- Classrooms are supportive of literacy development generally
- Teachers are aware of literacy issues and manage classroom opportunities for literacy development generally
- Teachers make purposeful use of time in discrete literacy lessons established as part of the project
- The project in practice follows a needs identification and address model which includes auditing, implementing, monitoring and evaluating the school's work
- Any intervention strategy is felt to work by those involved, including the students who are participating
- The LEA supports the project in practice in each of the schools taking part.

Eleven key issues arising from the projects

Of the twenty issues the HMI inspection identified as arising from its inspection of the Key Stage 3 projects, the following 11 are the most generally applicable to schools outside of the project considering whole-school approaches to literacy:

- What is meant by a literate Key Stage 3 or secondary age student? How does this differ from the definition provided in the Literacy Framework for eleven year olds?
- Is literacy development for all? What are the particular needs of boys, EAL students and higher attainers? How should they best be met?
- Where does literacy development fit within the Key Stage 3 curriculum? What is its relationship to English and to existing SEN work?
- How is transfer of learning best facilitated across the curriculum?
- What is the relationship between literacy development and improving standards of speaking and listening?
- What strategies should there be for monitoring and evaluating literacy development? How do monitoring and evaluation encompass aspects of value-addedness?
- What levels of knowledge about language do teachers need? What implications are there for the training of teachers?
- How, if at all, should the Key Stage 2 Framework be linked to literacy development at Key Stage 3?
- How aware are secondary phase teachers of literacy developments at Key Stages 1 and 2?
- What is the cost of any intervention strategy in terms of financial outlay and 'on costs'? How effective is it?
- To what extent is education prepared for the new literacies of the 21st century and, in particular, the impact of information and communication technology (ICT) on reading and writing?

The Ofsted remit for literacy at Key Stage 3

The following ten points are considered by Ofsted:

- The problems that the survey schools are facing and the costs of meeting them.
- The account taken by secondary schools of Key Stage 2 test data and the means by which assessments of attainment on entry are made.
- How much and what kind of reading and writing, in class and at home, is being done in a range of subjects.
- Expenditure on books and the quality and quantity of books available.
- The characteristics of good direct teaching of reading and writing in key subjects.
- The effectiveness of work by special educational needs and language support teams.
- The use of specific interventions such as paired reading, volunteer tutoring and after-school activities.
- What is done to promote independent reading for pleasure and information, including effective steps taken to encourage boys in particular.
- The use made of school and public libraries.
- The contribution made by the use of information and communication technology.

The HMI form for considering literacy

Below is the HMI form used for considering the effectiveness of secondary school approaches to literacy (from the secondary literacy exercise, Autumn Term 1998).

Form A: HMI

1 School:

2 Type and status:

3 LEA:

4 Age range:

5 Context (socio-economic background, ethnicity, EAL and bilingualism and other relevant matters).

6 Attainment of students on entry (brief details) and use to which the information (KS2 tests, other assessment records) is put by heads of department and class teachers.

7 Rationale: what is the nature of the school's approach to literacy and what are the intended outcomes of its work in this area? How has the need been identified? What costs are involved (money, time, resources)?

8 Nature of any literacy initiative/intervention/project/approach taken. When did it begin? Please describe briefly.

9 What, specifically, does the school do to help those students who enter year 7 with a depressed performance in reading and writing?

10 Management: who is responsible for the development of students' literacy and to whom is that person or group accountable?

11 Which departments or other groups are involved?

12 Which students are involved? Please list the target groups.

13 How does the school evaluate the outcomes of its work on literacy?

14 Documentation: please indicate what information about the work is readily available and include examples of key documentation if possible (e.g. school development plan, language policy, references in subject policy documents, information for parents).

15 What preparation/INSET has been necessary for staff?

16 Please give details of any external support or guidance (e.g. LEA, consultant, HE).

17 Summary (brief comments – refer to previous questions)

Strengths: Weaknesses:

18 Overall judgement to aid retrieval (please tick):
  A Very effective
  B Many effective features
  C Some effective features
  D Not an effective approach

Appendix 2 Example literacy audit

The following is an example of how one school carried out a literacy audit.

Literacy Working Party Report To The Governors

The initial brief

- To consider a whole-school policy for developing literacy and oracy.
- To produce a statement of entitlement for students ensuring that they have the literacy and oracy skills to give them access to all areas of the curriculum.
- To audit and disseminate good practice and strategies for developing literacy and oracy.
- To promote literacy and oracy skills.
- To consider how whole-school initiatives can provide and support literacy and oracy skills.

The group's basic premise

- To remind all staff that they each have a responsibility for developing literacy.
- To assume that all subjects in school should help students to develop their language skills because language is at the heart of the learning process.

The starting point

Our starting point was to research our students' actual experience of literacy in order to find out what is actually going on in school. We examined the Ofsted Report and found at least 30 references to literacy across a wide range of subjects and curriculum areas. Ofsted's conclusions were that:

- Deficiencies in basic literacy restrict effective learning
- Deficiencies in basic literacy and numeracy undermine attainment for many
- The standards of basic literacy are often insufficient to allow students to make appropriate headway throughout the curriculum
- Samples of students' work in Key Stage 3 were examined in order to comprehend, not only the nature of the problem, but also how poor, or underdeveloped, literacy skills were affecting students' achievement in two National Curriculum areas, English and Science.

The audit

It was felt that the next task for the working party was to undertake a thorough whole-school audit of the literacy demands which are made upon students, and the range and purposes of literacy that students experience.

The audit was in three stages:

1 An examination of the texts, reading materials and worksheets that Year 7 students have used during the first half of this term
2 A reading survey to all departments requesting information on a range of reading materials, approaches to developing reading strategies and differentiation
3 Shadowing of individual Year 7, 8 and 9 students throughout the curriculum to record the literacy demands being made upon students in a typical day and how individuals were coping with them.

Initial observations

Although complete reports on our findings so far are still in the process of being written up, some initial observations are:

- Some materials are demanding reading skills of a very high order
- Students need to be taught how to use reference materials and have easy access to them
- There is a need for INSET on worksheet design
- Reading in order to acquire information is a reading skill that needs to be taught
- The range of texts students encounter is minimal; the purposes of reading are rarely made explicit
- Little work is being undertaken to develop the reading levels of the more able
- Information from the Special Needs Department is recorded but rarely used to inform planning – more help is needed here
- The amount of examination practice and preparation which students experience is limited
- Out of 21 lessons observed, only two text books were seen and used
- There is wide use of blackboards and worksheets as a direct result of lack of text book resources
- The best lessons were when teachers differentiated their language to explain the nature of the work to all students.

The final audit report

The final audit report will highlight good practice and areas for action and will be used as a basis for many of the working party's recommendations.

The working party has now reached the stage where it is refining its definition of literacy and its purposes and is beginning to 'unwrap' what a literacy entitlement will mean in practice. It is proposed to clearly outline the rights of the students and the responsibilities of staff and parents and to make this information available in a variety of forms appropriate to the differing audiences. A uniformity of approach will be clearly outlined when recommendations are made for developing and teaching reading, writing, presentation, handwriting, subject-specific and Standard English, oracy, spelling and grammar.

It is envisaged that considerable whole-school and departmental INSET will be required to implement and monitor these policies if the working party's recommendations for whole-school initiatives are to be actively supported and owned by staff.

Appendix 3 Boys and achievement: does gender make a difference?

There has been much emphasis in recent years on boys' relative underachievement compared to girls'. Below are some suggested ways forward, plus a summary of the Government's response, some statistics and other background information.

Resources

The following three publications all contain very useful information on how to intervene effectively to improve boys' achievement.

- *Can Do Better* – booklet produced by QCA on practical suggestions for improving boys' enthusiasm for and attainment in English (tel: 0171 509 5555).
- *SCAA Boys and English Starter Pack* – a collection of articles and information to help teachers to start thinking about boys' achievement in English in their schools, plus some ideas for practical approaches in the classroom. Contact QCA (tel. 0171 509 5555).
- *Improving Boys' Literacy*, by Graham Frater – a survey of effective practice in secondary schools. Contact Basic Skills Agency (tel. 0171 405 4017).

The summary of the main findings in *Improving Boys' Literacy* states that the policies that were especially effective involved:

- Scrupulous baseline testing of all students
- Targeting, monitoring and mentoring of individual students
- Explicit attention to teaching quality as a whole-school issue
- The explicit development, usually through in-service training, of the staff's awareness of boys' needs
- Motivating boys.

It is also worth remembering the findings of research at Sheffield University, on Template 7, page 21, that list the approaches found to be effective in improving boys' performance.

What to do about it

You may wish to set up a working party just focusing on maximising boys' achievement. Alternately, you could decide that if the research findings are right, and since these would also appear to be a list of effective teaching processes, all of which are literacy related, you may wish to leave this as a strand within your whole-school approach. All aspects of the policy will need considering in the light of the needs of different groups of students, whether they be of a particular gender, ethnic or intelligence grouping. Some students may well fall into several such categories, for example, an underachieving, potentially very gifted boy with EAL needs who happens not to be interested in football. The working party will need to keep the interests of a whole range of groups in mind.

Using interest as a motivating factor is undoubtedly a good way in. Appendix 4, pages 126–136, contains the outline of a unit of work designed in the mode of the literacy hour, using the Year 5 targets. It uses text related to football in order to motivate boys (and girls) to improve their literacy.

You may wish to include the following practical approaches, adapted from Peter Traves' work at Wakeman School, Shropshire, on raising boys' achievement, within the scope of your working party

Questioning your perceptions

- What are your perceptions of the differences in achievement between boys and girls in your school?
- Are these perceptions based on:
  - Research?
  - Common-sense?
  - Analysis of results?
  - Anecdote?
  - Observation – casual or systematic?
- What action has been taken in response to these perceptions?
- What further action might be worth considering?

Getting information on which to base your way forward

- **Analyse results** Look in detail at cohorts of boys and girls to see precise differences in performance at GCSE. You may also wish to consider ethnicity.
- **Target a small group of boys** in the middle/upper range of ability who have suspect motivation, and sample their work, observe them in lessons and interview them. You may wish to target a similar group of girls.
- **Sample work** Select a range of types of writing and consider:
  - The standard of performance
  - The teacher's written response.
- **Conduct interviews** These can help establish:
  - Boys' attitudes to speaking and listening, reading and writing – what they enjoy and what they are doing well in, as well as what they dislike
  - Responses to different kinds of work, teaching, marking and teacher response
  - Areas of concern and targets to concentrate on over the next few weeks.
- **Observe lessons** Look for differences in the working habits and attitudes of boys and girls.
- **Use questionnaires** The results help teachers identify students' approaches to work, work habits, levels of performance, etc. and can then be used to negotiate targets with students. See the example of a questionnaire on Template 76, page 125.

Presenter's notes

Propose to your working party that a small group of underachieving boys is targeted as suggested above. Use the questionnaire on Template 76 to help discover if the group has similar approaches to work. Use the results to draw up suggestions to help teachers teach underachieving boys more successfully.

The key purpose of the questionnaire is to help construct individual targets for the boys to help them move forward. The individual attention that such an approach entails will have a positive effect in its own right, as any teachers who have been involved with individual interviews and related individual action planning with students will know.

Some possible remedies

Monitoring Identify students early who would benefit from being checked up on. It needs to be a relatively small group if it is to be manageable. This monitoring should include:

☐ Homework diary checked regularly
☐ Homework checked for completion on time and quality – failure followed up rapidly
☐ Close scrutiny of classwork and attitude in class – shortcomings quickly followed up
☐ Half-termly interview considering work.

Setting short-term targets The Ofsted report on boys in English reiterates the Sheffield University finding that boys respond to the setting of clear short-term targets. Is there scope for more units to be organised into sub-sections that need to be completed by a set date? For example, tightly structured tasks and materials that take them through the process step by step and that allow for the setting of deadlines.

More flexible grouping arrangements Ensure that grouping arrangement are more flexible.

The Government's response

The national context

☐ At Key Stages 2 and 3 girls significantly outperform boys in both reading and writing.
☐ At Key Stages 2 and 3 the gap in levels of achievement for boys and girls shows no sign of closing.
☐ The level of boys' achievement at reading and writing gives cause for concern.

In January 1998 the Government launched action to prevent the gap between girls' and boys' achievement at school level from widening. Each education authority is required to have plans to tackle boys' underachievement.

In February 1999 money was made available to encourage primary schools in England to hold extra writing lessons, particularly for boys who were liable to fail by a narrow margin to reach the level expected of them in the summer 1999 SATs. The focus was on guided writing. Students were to be encouraged, kept on task and offered work based on non-fiction, which is normally preferred by boys.

Researchers at Cambridge University have been commissioned by Ofsted to look at why boys have fallen behind over the past 10 years, and to report on what schools and local authorities are doing to address this.

Some more statistics on boys' underachievement

☐ Girls continue to out-perform boys, with 51.5 % of girls achieving five or more GCSE grades A* to C, compared with 41.3% of boys in 1998. But results vary greatly from area to area. For example, in Croydon, south London, 48% of girls achieved five or more high grade GCSEs as opposed to 33% of boys, whereas their near neighbour, Sutton, achieved figures of 54% for boys and 56% of girls achieving the equivalent level.
☐ The gap is widest for English, with 59% of girls achieving grade C or better compared with just 41% of boys. Of the 50,000 students leaving school without any qualifications, 28,500 are boys (57%).
☐ According to guidance sent to schools by the DfEE, at seven, 21% of girls reach National Curriculum Level 3 in English, compared with just 14% of boys. At 11, Level 4 is reached by 69% of girls but 57% of boys; at 14, Level 5 is reached by 66% of girls as opposed to 47% of boys.
☐ Four decades ago girls were doing better than boys in the 11-plus examination, requiring education administrators to set a lower cut-off point for boys to ensure equal numbers of each gender went on to grammar schools.
☐ Three-quarters of mothers read with their children when they are aged between five and seven, but only half of fathers do so.

Viewpoints on boys' underachievement

☐ Girls' underachievement in maths and science was focused on in the seventies and eighties. It could be that it is not boys who are doing worse than before, but girls who are steadily doing better. Girls are now taking maths and science in much larger numbers since they are now compulsory subjects. Greg Brookes of the NFER, who has examined gender differences in education, commented:

'Girls have always done better, but the gap is more marked now than ever before. Boys tended to catch up in secondary schools, but increasingly over the last 10 to 15 years the girls have been staying ahead.'

☐ The world of work, particularly for the working class, is changing rapidly. Manufacturing jobs are declining rapidly, while information and leisure jobs are on the increase.
☐ Others point out that the statistical under-achievement of boys in school is nothing compared with the statistical over-achievement of men in life. An editorial in *The Guardian* highlighted the fact that everyone needs to improve, not just the boys.

Research warns against giving dogs bad names

Teachers' attitudes have a significant effect on boys' achievement, according to the NFER's report *Boys' Achievement, Progress, Motivation and Participation* (May 1999). Too many strategies are put in place based on untested assumptions, with little regard for what boys really think, do and feel. No firm evidence exists that the gap between boys' and girls' English performance reflects a difference in innate linguistic ability.

Teachers are in a position to contradict or reinforce negative stereotyping that can label some students, particularly boys, low achievers from an early age. Staff should have high expectations of all students and stereotypes must be challenged. The role of the teacher is particularly highlighted in influencing boys' propensity to read, as well as their choice of reading.

Identifying approaches to work

Key to grading: 1 is the most positive

| Name: | Form: |
| Date: | Teacher: |

Capacity, skill or work habit	Rating
Ability to grasp new concepts	1 2 3 4
Ability to communicate concepts	1 2 3 4
Quality of oral contribution	1 2 3 4
Quality of presentation of work	1 2 3 4
Usually completes set tasks to acceptable standard	1 2 3 4
Capacity to follow instructions	1 2 3 4
Sustains concentration	1 2 3 4
Ability to use initiative	1 2 3 4
Enthusiasm for work	1 2 3 4
Ability to settle to task	1 2 3 4
Organisational skills	1 2 3 4
Meets homework deadlines	1 2 3 4

Comments

....

....

....

....

....

....

Key targets for improvement

1

2

3

4

Appendix 4 Football unit – overview

(NLS objective: W: 3, 8; S: 3, 4, 6, 8, 9; T: 21, 22, 24, 25, 26) The following unit of work is designed to fit in with some of the non-fiction framework objectives for Year 5, Term 1, and related strands indicated above. If you look in the literacy framework you will see that all the different elements of the Word, Sentence and Text strand for each term are numbered to aid planning. The text and tasks are all related to football. It could be differentiated to suit a wide range of abilities. Where text is to be read and introduced initially by the teacher, challenging text has been selected. The work particularly focuses on recount writing through using and constructing planning and writing frames of increasing complexity, as well as talking through and discussing the processes.

Presenter's notes

Below is an overview of the unit, followed by lesson plans and related handouts for most of the lessons (see pages 127–136).

A few lessons have been omitted because of lack of space. This unit of work is included to provide the English department with examples of planning in the mode of the literacy hour for students who need to reinforce skills that would move them from Level 3 to Level 4. It includes examples of how to involve students in the planning process for structuring their writing.

Lesson 1 Information
Reading for information, including understanding tables and diagrams
(Not included in handbook.)

Objectives To reinforce ability to extract appropriate information from tables and diagrams, including understanding abbreviations and selecting the evidence to support answers. To recognise the assumptions text makes about existing knowledge.

Text selected A football club fixtures' programme.
Advice for teacher Get hold of a football fixtures' programme for any appropriate football club. Look at the text/diagrams/timetables provided and work out a series of questions to discuss with the class about the presentation and nature of the text. Remember to include all the assumptions that the text makes about the reader's knowledge of football, the club etc. Create an OHP slide of one side of the programme so that you can focus attention on the aspects you want to highlight. Devise a series of questions about the text that the students have to work on in groups. The plenary session should focus more on the evidence for the answers than the answers themselves.

Lesson 2 Giving clear instructions
Objectives To reinforce and make explicit familiarity with procedural language – the language of instruction. To reinforce appropriate use of the imperative, including the ability to follow and give clear instructions orally and in written form using appropriate phrases, connectives and clauses in chronological order. To revise the use of capital letters for proper nouns. To proof-read work.

Text selected An extract from A–Z and related instructions. (See pages 127–129.)

Lesson 3 Introducing/reviewing recount writing
Objectives To revise the general features of recount writing including structure, language features and style (focusing on past tense, connectives and use of first person, description, vocabulary, use of speech). To write own recount using appropriate structure and style.

Text selected Autobiographical recount writing. (See pages 130–131.)

Lesson 4 Recount writing – blurbs
Objectives To understand the structure of recount writing and how it relates to audience and purpose – in this case a book blurb. To build awareness of structure by being involved in the process of constructing own recount writing frame for a book blurb and then writing blurb in appropriate structure and style. To revise/introduce punctuation to indicate an interruption of thought or direction, and to revise use of capital letters. To proof-read work.

Text selected Book blurb. (See pages 132–133.)

Lesson 5 Looking at different types of recount
(Not included in handbook.)

Objectives To reinforce understanding of how text is structured to suit particular purpose and audience (e.g. Internet) and presentation of evidence to support viewpoint.

Text selected Extract from a football club website.
Advice for teacher any appropriate football website, e.g. www.whufc.co.uk for West Ham United or www.heartsfc.co.uk for Heart of Midlothian, and find a page written by a footballer. Select one with a clear recount structure to it, then use this text as a sequencing exercise. In groups, the students have to sequence the text and then write the planning frame to support it, plus establish the key conventions of recount writing. They could also discuss what is different about the text because it was written for the Internet. Use the plenary session to draw out the key elements of recount writing.

Lesson 6 Recount writing – tabloid newspaper articles
Objectives To consider how tabloid newspapers present the sports news and the effects this has on the presentation of text, including use of headlines, the language of headlines, sub-headings, images, use of abbreviations and emotive language. To build understanding of technical terms relating to newspaper text.

Text selected Back page of tabloid newspaper. (See pages 134–135.)

Lesson 7 Writing your own recount articles
Objectives To apply knowledge about structure and content of article writing. (Relate to lesson 3 – the same event could be the content of the article.) To draft an article focusing on appropriate structure and presentation of content, given purpose and audience, e.g. something to hook the reader, use of quotations and eye-catching heading. To read through for structure and content. Redraft and proof-read for accuracy. (See page 136.)

Lesson 2 Giving clear instructions

NLS objective: Year 5, Term 1, Strand T2, T25; S9, S3.

Providing information

Objectives
- [ ] To reinforce and make explicit familiarity with procedural language – the language of instruction.
- [ ] To reinforce appropriate use of the imperative, including the ability to follow and give clear instructions orally and in written form using appropriate phrases, connectives and clauses in chronological order.
- [ ] To revise the use of capital letters for proper nouns.
- [ ] To proof-read work.

Teacher's notes
Part 1 (15 minutes) – introduce objectives

Explain that the lesson will focus on giving clear instructions. Write all street names in advance on the board so that spelling street names does not impede the activity. Remind the class to use capital letters for all these proper nouns.

Craven Cottage	Bishop's Park Road
Bishop's Park	Finlay Street
River Thames	Eternity Walk
Stevenage Road	Inglethorpe Street
Woodlawn Road	Kenyon Street
Fulham Palace Road	

Everyone is given a map of the area around Craven Cottage without any of the street names filled in (left-hand side of Template 78, page 129). The class listens while the text explaining the layout of the streets around Fulham's football ground at Craven Cottage is read out (Template 77, page 128). The whole text should be read through once at normal speed and then again, very slowly to allow students time to fill in the map according to the information they have heard.

After the second read-through, the students check their maps against the original (right-hand side of Template 78, now on OHP) and correct any errors.

Part 2 (25 minutes) – oral task

With the map still on the OHP, ask the class to give the instructions below orally. Draw attention to the appropriate use of language to express clear directions. Draw the class's attention to the list of useful expressions below, which could be displayed on the wall or the board. (If you are using a whiteboard as your screen, the phrases/clauses could be written down the side of the board so that they are visible but not cutting across the map text.)

Useful phrases and clauses

Introduce the following phrases and clauses, reinforcing them within the discussion and encouraging students to use them.
- [ ] take the first turn
- [ ] on the left
- [ ] on the right
- [ ] carry straight on
- [ ] on your right
- [ ] on your left
- [ ] ahead of you
- [ ] the road bears left
- [ ] at the crossroads
- [ ] follow the road round
- [ ] directly opposite
- [ ] diagonally opposite
- [ ] at the first set of traffic lights
- [ ] go straight ahead
- [ ] continue until

While the speaker gives the instructions, ask another student to point out where the person is being directed to (whether right or wrong) by following the instructions exactly as they are spoken.

Instructions
- [ ] Give directions to someone who is standing outside Craven Cottage who wants to get to the post office.
- [ ] Tell someone who is standing on the corner of Bishop's Park Road and Fulham Palace Road how they can get to the sports centre.
- [ ] Give directions to someone who is on Fulham Palace Road, on the corner of Bishop's Park Road, who wants to get to the sports centre.

Extend this activity by asking students to pretend they are talking to a visitor to the school who needs clear directions about how to get from one part of the school to another. Ask the listeners to check for the accuracy and clarity of these directions and suggest improvements. Keep the session going until you feel the students have progressed in their ability to give clear directions. (This may need revisiting on a regular basis until the appropriate instructions become very familiar to the group.)

Part 3 (10 minutes) – written task

Set the class the following task: 'Using your map, write directions for the following. Check that your directions are clear and that you have used capital letters appropriately.'
- [ ] Explain how someone can get from the corner of Bishop's Park Road and Stevenage Road to Kenyon Street.
- [ ] Explain how someone can get from the corner of Kenyon Street and Stevenage Road to the school on Finlay Street.
- [ ] Explain how someone who has got off the bus on Fulham Palace Road by Kenyon Street can get to Craven Cottage.
- [ ] Give directions to someone on Eternity Walk who wants to get to the post office.

Ask students to write clear instructions explaining how someone would get from their home to school.

Part 4 Ten-minute review
- [ ] Ten minutes before the end of the lesson, ask the class to read their answers through carefully, correcting them as appropriate (checking for clarity, use of capital letters, etc.), and then write a brief comment about how well they think they have completed the task.
- [ ] Ask some students to read out their answers – the class discusses which answers are the clearest, and why.
- [ ] Start building up a word wall for this unit:
  procedural writing   directions   sequence
  imperative   instructions   chronological   clarity
  confusion   diagonally   accuracy

Craven Cottage

The River Thames is the strip along the left side of the map. Craven Cottage, Fulham FC, is at the north end of Bishop's Park to the right of the River Thames. There is a grid pattern of streets next to the club. The first street running parallel to the river is Stevenage Road. The next street parallel to that is called Woodlawn Road. This street is parallel to the main road, Fulham Palace Road. The road at the southern end of the grid is called Bishop's Park Road. If you walk up Stevenage Road from Bishop's Park Road, the fourth road on your right is called Finlay Street. If you walk up Finlay Street, the building to your left is a school.

To the north of the football ground there is a dead-end road called Eternity Walk. The building on the north corner of that street and Stevenage Road is a sports centre.

The road opposite the entrance to Eternity Walk is Inglethorpe Street. Continue all along Inglethorpe Street and turn left on to Fulham Palace Road. The first road to your left is Kenyon Street. A few yards down this street on the left-hand side is the post office.

Giving clear instructions

Map of streets around Craven Cottage, Fulham FC

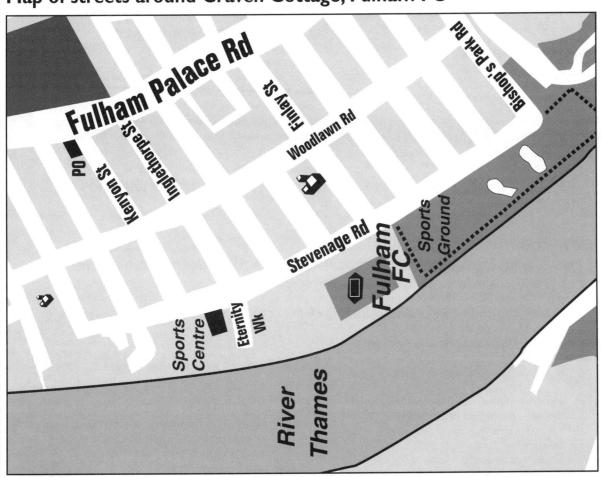

Lesson 3 Introducing/reviewing recount writing

NLS objective: Year 5, Term 1, Strand T21, T24; S8, S3.

Recount writing using autobiographical text

Objectives

☐ To revise the general features of recount writing, including structure, language features and style (focusing on past tense, connectives and use of first person, description, vocabulary, use of speech).

☐ To write own recount using appropriate structure and style.

☐ To work out meaning of difficult vocabulary from context.

Teacher's notes

Part 1 (20 minutes) – introduce objectives

Using an OHP, read the passage from Nick Hornby's *Fever Pitch* (Template 79, page 131) and discuss the following:

☐ **Structure** What structure has the writer chosen for this piece of writing? Is it chronological?

☐ **Tense** Most of this recollection of the writer's first visit to a football match is in the past tense. Why do you think he chose to write the actual description of the game in the present tense?

☐ **Direct speech** Near the end of the passage, the writer uses some direct speech (the actual words spoken). Who is speaking? How do we know it is the actual words that were spoken by the men?

☐ **Emphasis** When the writer really wants to stress his words, what does he do?

☐ **Person** What features suggest that this writing is autobiographical? What else could it be?

☐ **Descriptive style** What helps the reader build up a vivid picture of the event?

☐ **Vocabulary** Consider some of the difficult words that can be understood through context, e.g. recalls, enables, incomprehensible, reliable, overwhelming, awed, entire.

Part 2 (10 minutes) – language task

Distribute copies of the text to the group (one between two).

☐ Working in pairs, students highlight all the phrases or sentences in the passage that they think work well.

☐ They underline any words that they think help paint a picture of the event in their mind.

Part 3 (20 minutes) – writing task

☐ Set the students the following task: 'Write your own memories of any football match, music concert or event that you have been to that you particularly remember. Try to make your writing as vivid as possible. Don't try to cover everything, but select the most entertaining or interesting points. You may want to use this writing frame to help you get going and to structure your memories'.

Writing frame checklist

■ The .... that I remember best was ....

■ The reason why this has stayed in my memory is ....

■ One of the best moments was ....

■ As I left, I felt ....

☐ Fifteen minutes before end of lesson, ask the students to read their stories through, check them carefully, correcting their draft as appropriate, and then write a brief comment about how well they think they have completed the task.

Part 4 Ten-minute review

☐ Ask some students to read out the beginning of their story – the class discusses whether the structure and style are appropriate and effective.

They then decide on the typical features of recount writing.

☐ Add to the unit's word wall:
recount   autobiographical   connectives   structure
context   recollection   past tense   direct speech
first person   style

An extract adapted from *Fever Pitch*, by Nick Hornby

Nick Hornby recalls the first football match he went to watch at the Arsenal in 1968 when he was aged eleven.

I don't recall much about the football that first afternoon. One of those tricks of memory enables me to see the only goal clearly: the referee awards a penalty (he runs into the area, points a dramatic finger, there's a roar); a hush as Terry Neill takes it, and a groan as Gordon Banks dives and pushes the ball out; it falls conveniently at Neill's feet and this time he scores. But I'm sure this picture has been built up from what I have long known about similar incidents and actually I was aware of none of this. All I really saw on the day was a bewildering chain of incomprehensible incidents, at the end of which everyone around me stood and shouted. If I did the same it must have been an embarrassing ten seconds after the rest of the crowd.

But I do have other, more reliable, and probably more meaningful memories. I remember the overwhelming maleness of it all – cigar and pipe smoke, foul language (words I had heard before, but not from adults, not at that volume), and only years later did it occur to me that this was bound to have an effect on a boy who lived with his mother and sister; and I remember looking at the crowd more than at the players. From where I was sitting I could probably have counted twenty thousand heads. My father told me there were nearly as many people in the stadium as lived in my town, and I was suitably awed.

It wasn't the size of the crowd that impressed me most, however, or the way adults were allowed to shout obscene words as loudly as they wanted without attracting any attention. What impressed me most was just how much most of the men around me hated, really hated, being there. As far as I could tell, nobody seemed to enjoy, in the way that I understood the word, anything that happened during the entire afternoon. Within minutes of the kick-off there was real anger: "You're a DISGRACE, Gould. He's a disgrace!"

"A hundred quid a week? A HUNDRED QUID A WEEK! They should give that to me for watching you."

As the game went on, the anger turned into outrage and then seemed to curdle into sullen, silent discontent. Yes, yes, I know all the jokes. What else could I have expected at Highbury? But I went to Chelsea and to Tottenham and to Rangers, and saw the same thing: that the natural state of the football fan is bitter disappointment, no matter what the score.

Lesson 4 Recount writing – blurbs

NLS objective: Year 5, Term 1, Strand T21, T24; S6; W8.

The structure of the blurb at the front of a book

Objectives

☐ To understand the structure of recount writing and how it relates to audience and purpose – in this case a book blurb. To work out the meaning of new vocabulary from context and roots.

☐ To build awareness of structure by being involved in the process of constructing own recount planning frame for a book blurb and then writing blurb in appropriate structure and style.

☐ To revise/introduce punctuation to indicate an interruption of thought or direction and to revise the use of capital letters.

☐ To proof-read work.

Teacher's notes

Part 1 (10 minutes) – introduce objectives

Using an OHP of the text from the inside cover of the book *Left Foot in the Grave* by Garry Nelson (Template 80, page 133), discuss with the class the meaning of blurb and its purpose and audience, as well as ways of coping with new vocabulary from context (e.g. crossroads, journeyman, acclaim, marketing, perennial[1], temperamental, ironic, clamber, contemporary[2], bandwagon, veteran footsoldier, fledgling). Blurbs are a form of recount writing, since they are an account of the content of a book, but as their purpose is to persuade as well as inform they have some of the elements of persuasive text in them.

---

[1]Per = prefix usually meaning 'through', 'all over', as in pervade, perform, persist, perceive; annual — from latin for 'year'.

[2]Con = prefix that means 'with' or 'against'; tempus = Latin for 'time'.

Part 2 (20 minutes) – features to discuss

☐ **Tense** Why is it written in the past tense?

☐ **Author** Who wrote this blurb?

☐ **Punctuation to indicate hesitation** What punctuation does the writer use in the second paragraph to show that Garry Nelson was uncertain what to do next?

☐ **Use of italics** How can you quickly pick out any titles referred to in the text?

☐ **Assumptions about audience** The writer assumes readers will know what FIFA means. Why is this assumption made? What is FIFA? What other assumptions does the writer make about readers?

☐ **Persuasion** Which is the most persuasive sentence in the text? Where has it been placed?

☐ **Structure** Use the board to construct with the group the structure of the piece.

Part 3 (20 minutes) – writing exercise

☐ Set the students the following task: 'Write a blurb for any book that you know well. Try to make it a similar length to the blurb on *Left Foot in the Grave?* Use a similar four-paragraph structure. You may want to use this writing frame to help you get going and to structure your thoughts.'

> #### Writing frame checklist
>
> ■ Title: ....
>
> ■ "...................................." is set in
> ....
>
> ■ Your interest builds up when
> ....
>
> ■ You want to know what will happen when
> ....
>
> ■ Anyone who is interested in
> .... will love
> "...................................." because
> ....

☐ Fifteen minutes before end of lesson, ask the students to read their stories through, check them carefully, correcting their draft as appropriate, and then write a brief comment about how well they think they have completed the task.

Part 4 Ten-minute review

☐ Ask some students to read out the beginning of their blurb – the class discusses whether the structure and style are appropriate and effective.

☐ Remind the group what they had decided were the typical features of recount writing. Does their list need amending?

☐ Add to the unit's word wall:
blurb   audience   purpose   planning frame
hesitation   italics   assumption   persuasion

Book Blurb

Left Foot in the Grave? A view from the bottom of the Football League, by **Garry Nelson**

In the spring of 1996, Garry Nelson found himself at a crossroads in his career. *Left Foot Forward,* his account of a year in the life of a journeyman footballer, had brought him huge acclaim and bestseller status. But now his club Charlton Athletic were letting him go. After eighteen seasons as a professional player, he was out of a job.

A move into marketing?... Or journalism, perhaps?... Maybe even a small business? No, Nelson's love of the game would not let him walk away so easily. Even though, coming from the Football League's bottom club, an offer to join Torquay as player coach was one he couldn't refuse. No less resistible was the urge to begin charting the highs, if any, and the many lows of life down among football's perennial strugglers.

Overnight, Garry Nelson found himself both a player and a back room boy. With one foot in either camp, he now needed all his powers of observation. From temperamental mini-star and no-hoper reject through to the desperate search for players and the never-ending financial problem, this account of Torquay's struggle to rise from the grave, captures the essence of what English football is all about. As he takes in wider issues such as FIFA, England in Georgia and the funding of soccer, Nelson's sharp comparisons and ironic contrasts soon make it clear that he is writing not only about Torquay but about scores of English clubs, from the likes of Mansfield Town to Manchester United.

Left Foot in the Grave? is no fashionable attempt to clamber on the contemporary bandwagon of sports literature. Written by a veteran footsoldier still involved at the very heart of the game, a fledgling manager at the very bottom of the football pile, it communicates not how the beautiful game appears to the bystander but, simply, how it is – from the inside. English football has never been more authentically portrayed.

Lesson 6 Recount writing – tabloid newspapers

NLS objective: Year 5, Term 1, Strand T21; W8/3.

Presentation of tabloid newspaper articles

Objectives

- ☐ To consider how tabloid newspapers present the sports news and the effect this has on the presentation of text, including use of headlines, the language of headlines, sub-headings, images, use of abbreviations and emotive language.
- ☐ To build understanding of technical terms relating to newspaper text.
- ☐ To build vocabulary through identifying word roots and derivations.

Teacher's notes

Select the back page of any tabloid newspaper, preferably one that features a main sports article plus a few short taster articles to lure readers into the inside sports pages. You will also need Template 81, page 135.

Parts 1 and 2 (30 minutes) Introduce objectives

Present your chosen text to class on OHP and analyse its features. Introduce vocabulary from the list below. Relate it to roots, e.g. caption, capital, captain.

Newspaper technical vocabulary

Introduce the following terms and reinforce them within the discussion. Encourage students to use the appropriate terms when feeding back on their group's discussion. They should be added to your word wall.

- ☐ red top
- ☐ tabloid
- ☐ banner headline
- ☐ headline
- ☐ strapline
- ☐ caption
- ☐ column
- ☐ byline

Features to discuss

From your text:
- ☐ **Design/layout** Look at how much of the page is taken up by headlines, how much by pictures and how much by text. Why is this?
- ☐ **Layout** The back page probably includes the beginning of several articles, all of which are continued or further reported on inside pages. Why would the editor choose to do this? What is the effect of this on the reader?

From Template 81:
- ☐ **Headlines** Look at the banner headline. What is clever about it? On the same day (10th December, 1998) the *Sun* chose to write about the same match on its back page, using a very similar picture but using the headline "Squeezy does it!" Which do you think is better?

Look at the pun in the headline "The Roy's done good". Discuss what it stands for.

Underneath the headline is the strapline "Keane puts United into Euro last eight". Why do you think headline writers often also use straplines?

- ☐ **Quotation** The last three speech paragraphs are in Ferguson's words. How do we know this? Why aren't there marks at the end of the last complete paragraph?

Part 3 (15 minutes) – discussion

In small groups or pairs, students discuss the ideas and questions below and jot down their answers.

Looking at your chosen page, the students consider the following:
- ☐ List all the abbreviations used in the headlines on the back page
- ☐ Why do you think headlines tend to be made up of very short words and abbreviations?
- ☐ What does using such abbreviations assume about the readers?
- ☐ Decide on two other headlines that could have been used.

Looking at Template 81, the students consider the following:
- ☐ Roy Keane is the focus of the headline, the strapline and the picture, but he is not mentioned in the text underneath. Can you think of an explanation for this?
- ☐ Why has the journalist included words like 'ceasefire'?
- ☐ Why are the first words of the article in capital letters?

Part 4 (15 minutes) Review

Groups take it in turns to present their answers to one of the questions. The class discusses the answers and decides on the key features of the tabloid back page.

Mirror Sport · Mirror Sport · Mirror Sport · Mirror Sport · Mirror

THE ROY'S DONE GOOD

Keane puts United into Euro last eight

MAN UTD 1 BAYERN MUNICH 1   By DAVID MADDOCK

ALEX FERGUSON raised a glass to his German rivals last night as he toasted another glorious passage into the European Cup quarter-finals.

The Manchester United boss was left sweating towards the end of a tense contest with Bayern as qualification hung in the balance. With United only drawing, they desperately needed results elsewhere to go their way in order to slip through the back door of second place in Group D.

Incredibly, as Ferguson strained to learn of scores in other groups, he was put out of his misery by Bayern's players. They defied the history between these two nations, to call a ceasefire during the last five minutes of a game that was intensely fought before then.

A draw, of course, meant the Germans won the group, but it also allowed United a safe passage.

And Ferguson admitted that it was the Germans who told him his side were through – as they played out the draw.

"In the last five minutes there was no doubt in my mind we were through – because the Germans told me," he explained.

"The Germans are never wrong on these things, they always have the best information, and they let us know.

"It was incredible, you know, the

TURN TO PAGE 66

(from the *Mirror*, December 10, 1998)

Lesson 7 Writing your own recount

NLS objective: Year 5, Term 1, Strand T24; S3, S4.

Writing your own article

Objectives

- ☐ To apply knowledge about structure and content of article writing (relate to Lesson 3 pages 130-131 – the same event could be the content of the article).
- ☐ To draft an article, focusing on appropriate structure and presentation of content given the purpose and audience of the article, e.g. something to hook the reader, use of quotations and eye-catching heading.
- ☐ To read through for structure and content.
- ☐ To redraft and proof-read for accuracy.

Teacher's notes

Part 1 (15 minutes) Introduce objectives

Write the news article planning frame opposite on the board or on an OHP. Ask the students to write a magazine news article reporting on any school public event. It could be a sporting event, a music concert, a play or some sort of inter-group competition. If possible, select a recent school event that all students would be familiar with. This could be a rewrite of the autobiographical piece written for Lesson 3 for this new purpose and audience. You could then jointly construct a writing frame for the class to complement the planning frame below. The audience for this piece of writing would be the school community. Ensure that the class knows what assumptions they are writing within. Remind them that the audience won't want to read the article if it hasn't been made to seem interesting. Quotations are a useful way of livening up articles. Students should select an eye-catching heading, and possibly select some sub-headings to maintain interest.

Model for the class how to use this frame and jointly construct the beginning of an article.

Part 2 (20 minutes) Writing

Students write the first draft.

Part 3 (15 minutes) Read through

Students read through the article and adjust to increase impact, interest, etc. They check structure, then redraft and proof-read carefully. They then write a brief comment about how well they think they have completed the task.

Part 4 Ten-minute review

Students read out the first two paragraphs of their articles and discuss which are the most effective and why.

News-writing planning frame

1 Introductory paragraph

2 Paragraph for main news focus

(Check that you have included a **hook** to grab readers' interest, plus

who?

why?

when?

where?

and how? in these first two paragraphs)

3 Paragraph with less important news relating to main topic (include quotation about how a key character feels)

4 Paragraph with least important news relating to main topic

5 Final paragraph to act as a pointer – an end that suggests some sort of direction.

Appendix 5 ICT and literacy

More and more writing is now performed on computer than with pen and paper, while the Internet is used as the key source of information. Undoubtedly such developments will accelerate. Those who argue that the traditional core skills of reading and writing will suffer if too much emphasis is placed on ICT, miss the central point. Information and communication technology makes reading and writing more important, not less so. Composing on screen and accessing and searching for information through the Internet, or creating your own website actually require and develop reading and writing skills as well as changing them. E-mail facilitates conversational exchange based on reading and writing, while structuring a website and writing text suitable for reading on screen makes very significant new demands on the writer.

How much these technological changes will affect how and what we read and write is being researched currently, but clearly the medium by which you communicate affects how and what you communicate. To borrow Neil Postman's neat analogy, if the only medium of communication on offer were smoke signals, this would severely curtail the expression of philosophy. (Neil Postman's *Amusing Ourselves to Death* is a very interesting book on the difference television has made to a literate society, raising significant questions about how the way we communicates influences our culture.)

Schools are struggling to keep up with the pace and significance of ICT changes, not least because of the cost of the equipment and staff training. It is one thing to be computer literate; another to be able to integrate the use of ICT effectively into your teaching repertoire.

Schools have to worry about how they are going to get sufficient equipment; how they are going to train their staff and, most importantly, what their staff are going to do to with the equipment to enhance students' education.

Warning

Research has consistently shown that it is not sufficient just to provide teachers with the technology and training in how to use it. What is also required is training in what to do with the equipment to improve literacy; pedagogical guidance on how to teach using ICT.

This appendix covers:

☐ Low-cost versus state-of-the-art computers
☐ Potential advantages of word processors
☐ The advantages of ILS, the internet and CD-Roms
☐ Potential disadvantages of ICT
☐ Research: is there quantitative evidence that computers in schools raise standards in literacy?
☐ Exchanging information via the Internet
☐ Useful ICT-related publications

Low-cost versus state-of-the-art computers

It is worth bearing in mind that many students are provided with sophisticated computers that they only actually use as word processors. Schools may well wish to consider the multiple purchase of portable low-cost computers, to enable all students to have frequent access to word processing, rather than the purchase of much more expensive computers that are often systematically under-utilised. If the word processor route is contemplated, it is worth bearing in mind the following:

☐ Can you easily load text on to the machines so that all the class can be presented with material to work on?
☐ Is the screen a reasonable size, so that students can easily see a range of the text that they are creating rather than just two or three lines?

Potential advantages of word processors

☐ **Presentation** Work is legible and looks much more presentable. For those cursed with untidy handwriting it is much more fulfilling. It is far easier to read typed work, which aids discussion of how to improve text at word, sentence and text level.

☐ **Extended writing** The fact that work begun is easy to return to encourages extended writing even among very young students.

☐ **Redrafting to improve structure, expression and accuracy** The cut and paste facility is superb for redrafting work effectively. It enables far greater attention to be given to improving work at text, sentence and word level.

☐ **Working on pre-prepared text** The loading facility enables you to defeat the blank page/screen syndrome by scaffolding learning effectively. A wide range of text, writing frames or word banks can be presented for editing, sequencing, redrafting, composing and so forth.

☐ **Spelling** The spell-checking facility has its uses, especially if it is of the thesaurus variety that allows students to compare the spelling they used with a range of alternatives. However, it can lead to increased carelessness since spell-checkers only check that the word used is contained within its dictionary, not that it has been appropriately used in context. Moreover, students who lack confidence in their ability to spell will automatically assume that the machine knows best, rather than the fact that the spelling they used may correct, but not part of the machine's dictionary.

The following little ode to spell-checkers expresses their chief limitation rather neatly:

Spell Czech

I have a spelling chequer
Witch came with my pea see.
It plainly Marx for my revue
Miss steaks aye cannot sea.
I strike a quay or right a word
And weight for it to say
Whether eye am wrong or wright.
It shows me strait away.
As soon as a mist ache is maid,
It nose bee fore two late
And helps me put the error rite
Witches really rather grate.
I've run this poem threw it
I'm sure yore pleased to no.
Its letter perfect in it's weigh;
My chequer tolled me sew.

(adapted from an unknown source)

☐ **Grammar** Many people turn grammar-checkers off and refuse to use them. I would argue that they are a useful facility. You don't have to agree with it, but it's a useful check, not least on the tendency to write streams of complex sentences that Charles Dickens was rather better at than most of us.

The advantages of Integrated Learning Systems (ILS), the Internet and CD-ROMs

☐ **Teaching reading skills** Multimedia CD-ROMs, such as talking books or ILS, can offer interactive reading experiences that encourage the development of spelling skills, word recognition, vocabulary and comprehension. They can also help younger students make the links between objects, sounds and the letters that make up the words that denote the objects.

☐ **Providing research information** The Internet is an unrivalled source of information, with CD-ROMs also providing a great source of information.

☐ **Providing a sense of audience** Access to e-mail offers students a more realistic writing experience that can help develop a real sense of audience since students can genuinely communicate across the world with ease. Desk-top publishing software can also enhance this. The process of making a class newspaper is transformed.

☐ **Enhancing up-front teaching** Display technologies, such as large screens and electronic whiteboards, where the whole class can read and discuss a text and the teacher can model redrafting skills, could revolutionise the scope of direct teaching.

Potential disadvantages of ICT

☐ **Slowness due to lack of keyboard skills** Time needs to be allocated somewhere within the curriculum, but not in literacy time, to ensure that students use keyboards efficiently, otherwise hours of time will be wasted by slow keying in. Keying in is a useful technical skill, but it should not be confused with a literacy skill. The QCA scheme of work for ICT identifies appropriate activities for improving students' confidence with word processors, which often involve students redrafting text already provided for them. Such work focuses on reading and discussing text, not keying it in. One school I visited built keyboard skills into a unit of work in Year 7. Any student joining the school after this point was required to complete this unit.

It is easy to think that voice-activated computers instantly solve this problem, but as yet this technology brings a whole new series of problems. Even when these are resolved, people (teachers and students alike) will need significant training to adapt to the requirements of composing out loud. And, of course, it could make lessons rather noisy. But voice-activated software is definitely a magnificent advance for students with certain specific difficulties.

☐ **Lack of teacher knowledge** Be sure you are confident in what you are asking the class to do. Practise the task yourself and beware of pitfalls.

☐ **Increased carelessness** Students with a tendency not to read their work through can be even more careless when presenting work that has been word-processed, since their lack of skill in manipulating the keyboard may add to errors. Checking text and proof-reading need to be built into planning.

☐ **Endless fiddling with design rather than content** Don't allow the class to do any activity on the computer that you haven't agreed to. The clipart facilities and assorted fonts can lead to endless fiddling with titles, images and text, rather than actually getting on with a real writing task. If your class is working on networked computers, individuals can quietly access areas and entertainment very far from your planned lesson.

☐ **Endless printing (and printing bills)** Don't allow students to print anything they have not checked with you first.

☐ **Drowning in information** You can easily sink in the mass of information available on the Internet, or just download masses of undigested text. Copying has been taken to new levels.

☐ **Cheating** Computers and the Internet provide high-tech opportunities for presenting others' work as your own, with whole websites being dedicated to this purpose. It changes the territory for coursework.

☐ **Hacking into the system** Networked computers offer glorious opportunities for would-be hackers to practise the art of quiet vandalism. Don't leave any uninstall features on the start menu and install CD locks so that students, hopefully, can't install software. Schools need to consider how to prevent and deal with such problems.

Research

Is there quantitative evidence that computers in schools raise standards in literacy? There appears to be limited evidence that access to ICT raises levels of achievement. The two-year Exeter University project studied 11 schools in Bristol following the introduction of computers into the classroom. There was widespread anecdotal evidence of benefit to students. However, it did not provide conclusive evidence that the £4 million spent led directly to significant gains in literacy and numeracy.

Professor Niki Davis of the University of Exeter School of Education, who led the research, said 'Many teachers commented on the extension of the children's written and spoken vocabulary. One of the main successes has been the way that learning becomes more focused and information more shared'.

One school involved, St Pius Roman Catholic Primary, said it had seen a 20% improvement in its SATs scores at Key Stage 2 since the computers had been introduced. The head commented that he felt the computers had played a significant role in this but added, 'I would be loathe to say they are the sole factor.' He added that the biggest improvements had been in literacy, 'because they enjoy using the CD-ROMs and sending e-mails so much, they have far more motivation to read'.

Evaluation of ILS

An ILS system is a computer-based system that presents students with individual programmes of work over a number of weeks or months. The system can provide immediate feedback to students as they work, as well as detailed records on students' progress for teachers. Since 1993 BECTa (the British Educational Communications and Technology Agency) has evaluated the use of ILS in schools in the UK on behalf of the DfEE. The UK ILS *Evaluations – Final Report* is available from BECTa (01203 416669).

The key conclusions of this research are as follows:

☐ There is considerable evidence that students do learn from ILS. The main issue is not if students learn, but what and how they learn.

☐ The use of ILS has a marked positive effect on students' attitudes, motivation and behaviour. As yet evidence is inconclusive as to whether these positive impacts generalise beyond experience with ILS to influence more general attitudes towards schooling or school subjects.

☐ Where the use of ILS at least matches what can be achieved with conventional teaching, these systems offer a stimulating means of extending the range of learning opportunities open to students. However, the results suggest that exclusive reliance on ILS for preparation for Key Stage 3 tests and GCSE exams may have a negative impact, and imply that teaching by other methods is pedagogically necessary during the period of immediate preparation for these examinations.

☐ Although teachers and headteachers were generally positive in their attitudes towards ILS and their educational impact, there are issues to address concerning the apparent gap between the acquisition and evaluation of core skills and the wider knowledge and skills tested in examination performance.

☐ There was evidence from all three phases of evaluation that ILS can help to enhance teachers' confidence in IT and contribute to the development of their knowledge and skills in management and the use of educational technology.

Cut off by the technological tide

Nil by Mouth, a report commissioned by Anderson Consulting and Investors in People, found that 75% of communications were now conducted electronically. It highlighted two dangers:

☐ the increasing disenfranchisement of those not using technology

☐ information overload, with staff being targeted by huge volumes of unnecessary, poorly written, unfocused, ineffective messages.

Unsurprisingly, the report's first point is borne out by data from the *British Household Panel Study*, a yearly survey administered by the Institute for Social and Economic Research at Essex University. The distribution of home PCs is becoming increasingly skewed towards more well-off homes, putting children from poorer homes at a major disadvantage when it comes to accessing information technology. The greatest hope of rectifying this technological divide lies in the education system. Such findings provide a powerful argument for those who believe that greater investment in IT in schools is important in widening opportunities as well as improving skills.

It is true that faxes and e-mail mean that you can be inundated with unsolicited information. Moreover, e-mails and messages on websites are far more riddled with errors than letters received in the post. The send button seems to lure people into pressing it before checking the content of their messages.

Exchanging information via the Internet

'You might as well pin a message on the moon.' This was the reaction of one teacher in 1997 to the information that, from that meeting onwards, all communication was to be via the local Training and Enterprise Council's website. As the millennium approaches, many teachers still do not have easy workplace access to the Internet and some don't want it, but increasingly teachers are adapting to this amazing source of information and communication. The National Grid for Learning (www.ngfl.gov.uk), launched in October 1997, provides teachers with an excellent source of resources and information, as well as the facility to exchange ideas. Scotland (www.svtc.org.uk), England (www.vtc.ngfl.gov.uk) and Northern Ireland (www.nine.org.uk) now each has a Virtual Teacher Centre to support teaching, learning, training and administration in schools and colleges. The opportunity to exchange good ideas about teaching, including how to use ICT effectively, is now boundless. And, of course, e-mail communication is an excellent way of providing students with real audiences for their work.

Useful ICT publications

☐ Keep up to date with ICT information and research, and exchange ideas on www.becta.org.uk.

☐ The UK ILS *Evaluations – Final Report*, BECTa, 1997, tel. 01203 416669

☐ *History using IT: Improving Students' Writing in History using Word Processing*, BECTa (see above)

☐ Also see resources, page 144, for a whole range of useful websites.

Appendix 6 The role of school governors

The role of school governors in the development of your policy (adapted from Section 5 of *A Literacy Guide for School Governors*, National Literacy Trust).

All school governors will be aware that there is significant government focus on raising literacy standards. The publication of examination results and inspection reports, and the requirement for schools to set targets to improve their performance benchmarked against other comparable schools, mean that governors will know a lot more about their school's performance and will be asking questions about literacy standards in the school.

Governors must be kept informed of the school's approach to developing a whole-school literacy policy. They should to agree the literacy priorities for the school, and ensure they are incorporated into the school development plan. They will also want to be kept informed of the targets and evaluation of the policy.

Questions governors may ask

Initially
- Does the whole school community, including governors, challenge the level of aspirations and achievements of students?
- Is developing literacy across the curriculum seen as an issue for all students?
- Is the quality of student writing at a sufficiently high level to enable them to achieve their potential in examinations?
- What has the school done to make staff knowledgeable about the National Literacy Strategy?
- What is the school doing to ensure that the secondary curriculum builds on the primary experience of the students transferring?
- What use is made of primary school data on literacy?

On management
- Is a member of the senior management team responsible for the school literacy policy?
- What literacy staff training programme is planned?
- Is literacy on the agenda of departmental meetings?
- Is there a regular report to governors on progress in literacy across the curriculum?
- How is the school encouraging a coherent approach to teaching literacy in all curriculum areas and within tutor time?
- Each subject has its own vocabulary: is this specifically taught?
- Are students taught how to use reference materials? By whom?
- Can students use appropriate writing styles when, for example, presenting an argument, writing a report or writing up an experiment?
- Are subject teachers equipped to promote literacy skills? Has training been provided?

On students with literacy difficulties
- How is support provided for students with literacy difficulties?
- What system is in place for establishing which students need support?
- What systems are in place to ensure that subject teachers are aware of these students' difficulties?
- How is ICT used to support these students and boost their confidence and motivation?
- How does the SENCO review Individual Education Plans (IEPs) in the light of the literacy strategy?

On encouraging reading and writing for pleasure
- How does the school support reading for pleasure? How is literacy celebrated in the school?
- How does it use all appropriate resources (books, materials and displays, as well as electronic media) to promote reading and writing?
- Do parents attend reading and writing events or celebrations?
- Are students using the school library? Do Year 7 classes have library time? Does the range of books reflect the needs and interests of the students (especially boys)?
- What opportunities are there for governors to become involved in reading/writing events?

Governors' organisations
- Advisory Centre for Education (ACE) Ltd provides advice and publications for schools and parents. ACE, 1b Aberdeen Studios, 22–24 Highbury Grove, London N5 2DQ. Tel: 0171 354 8318; Fax: 0171 354 9069.
- Information for School and College Governors (ISCG) provides a free advice line with open access to all governors. It publishes checklists and reports on governor issues. It provides seminars for governing bodies in schools and LEAs and also runs larger conferences and conventions. Its representative Soundings Panel acts as a research panel on governor issues. ISCG, Avondale Park School, Sirdar Road, London W11 4EE. Tel: 0171 229 0200; Fax: 0171 229 0651.
- National Association of Governors and Managers (NAGM) offers an annual membership subscription to individual governors and governing bodies and provide a newsletter, general information, publications and access to an advice line. NAGM, 21 Bennets Hill, Birmingham B2 5QP Tel: 0121 643 5787.
- National Governors Council (NGC) is an independent forum for governing body associations in local education authorities, providing advice and support for governors and governing bodies. NGC, Glebe House, Church Street, Crediton, Devon, EX17 2AF Tel: 01363 774377 Fax: 01363 776007.

Appendix 7 Useful resources

From the National Literacy Trust

- ☐ Training courses and school INSET on *Raising achievement through whole-school approaches to literacy* – contact Julia Strong, tel. 0171 828 2435 (booking well in advance is normally essential).
- ☐ The National Literacy Trust's website. For information on secondary school initiatives, plus resources to support reading events, details of specialist children's bookshops and English as an additional language bookshops, and much more, look on the Trust's website: www.literacytrust.org.uk.
- ☐ *Literacy Today*, the National Literacy Trust's quarterly journal, regularly features articles about raising literacy standards in secondary schools. The September 1999 issue focuses on Key Stage 3.
- ☐ *Literacy Today Special* on the National Year of Reading, full of useful suggestions – free from the Trust.
- ☐ *A Literacy Guide for School Governors* – the role of school governors in raising literacy standards.
- ☐ A new set of posters depicting famous people, including footballers, promoting reading for pleasure. Available free courtesy of the NYR. Ring 0845 6022 260 and request order no. NYRP2.

Other useful resources

Government publications

- ☐ *Baseline Assessment for students starting primary school*, DfEE Circular 6/98.
- ☐ *Desirable outcomes for children's learning on entering compulsory education*, DfEE/QCA (1996).
- ☐ *Extending opportunity: a national framework for study support*, DfEE.
- ☐ *From targets to Action: guidance to support effective target setting in schools*. DfEE, 1997.
- ☐ *The Implementation of the National Literacy Strategy*, DfEE.
- ☐ *The Summer Literacy Schools: an evaluation of the 1998 pilot scheme* by Education Extra.
- ☐ *NLS Key Stage 3 Literacy Conferences, School file*, DfEE.
- ☐ *NLS: Guidance for providers of summer literacy schools and Key Stage 3 intervention programmes in literacy 1999–2000*, DfEE; tel. 0845 602 2260 quoting code SLSKS3.
- ☐ *NLS: Framework for Teaching*, DfEE, ISBN 085522 7141.
- ☐ *NLS: Literacy Training Pack – Primary*.

All DfEE publications are available from the DfEE's publications centre, Prolog, on 0845 6022260.

- ☐ *SCAA Use of Language: a common approach*. This includes an overall school document plus accompanying documents for each curriculum area. It is full of useful practical suggestions for improving teachers' awareness of language across the curriculum. Contact: QCA publications line, tel. 0171 509 5555.

Whole-school approaches

- ☐ *NATE Use of Language in the National Curriculum* (with guidance for developing a whole-school policy in secondary schools). Contact NATE, 50 Broadfield Road, Broadfield Business Centre, Sheffield S8 OXJ; tel. 0 1 14 25 5 5419; Fax: 0 1 14 25 5 5296.
- ☐ *Use of Language Across the Secondary Curriculum*, Eve Bearne (1998), Routledge, tel. 01264 343071.

- ☐ *Secondary teachers' views and actions concerning literacy and literacy teaching*, Maureen Lewis and David Wray (in press).
- ☐ Accelerated Learning has been recommended by many schools as augmenting their approach to literacy. *Accelerated Learning in Practice*, brain-based methods for accelerating motivation and achievement and *Accelerated Learning in the Classroom*, from the School Effectiveness series are both by Alistair Smith and are available from the Network Educational Press.

Non-fiction reading and writing

- ☐ *Extending Literacy – children reading and writing non-fiction*, David Wray and Maureen Lewis (Routledge). This excellent book looks at how children's skills are extended once they've achieved basic literacy and how effectively they interact with non-fiction books.

Writing frames

- ☐ *EXEL Writing Frames* and *Writing Across the Curriculum*. Excellent photocopiable material on writing frames. Contact: Reading and Language Information Centre, The University of Reading, Bulmershe Court, Earley, Reading RG6 1HY; tel. 01189 318820.
- ☐ *Analytical and Discursive Writing at Key Stage 3*, Christine Counsell, published by the Historical Association, tel. 01732 359 387.

Boys

- ☐ *SCAA Boys and English Starter Pack*. This is a useful collection of articles and information to help teachers start to think about boys' achievement in English in their schools, and includes some ideas for practical approaches in the classroom. Contact QCA, tel. 0171 509 5555.
- ☐ *Can Do Better* is a useful booklet produced by QCA on practical suggestions for improving boys' enthusiasm for and attainment in English. Tel. 0171 509 5555.
- ☐ *Improving Boys' Literacy* is a useful survey of effective practice in secondary schools (Graham Frater, Basic Skills Agency, 1997). To obtain a copy call 0870 600 2400.
- ☐ *Boys reading and writing* produced by Save the Children Fund, tel. 0171 700 8127.

Intervention programmes

- ☐ *What Works in Secondary Schools – Catching up with Basic Skills*. This is a very useful, practical analysis of effective practice in raising standards of basic skills. Contact the Basic Skills Agency, tel. 0171 405 4017.
- ☐ First Steps provides training in developing a literacy intervention strategy. See www.ghpd.co.uk or tel. 01865 314055.
- ☐ *Achieving dyslexia friendly schools* is an easy to read and practical resource pack produced by the British Dyslexia Association, tel. (admin.) 0118 966 2677; fax 0118 935 1927; Helpline 0118 966 8271.

Assessing progress in reading

- ☐ *Individualised Assessment of Children's Reading Development*. This has been developed by Birmingham LEA Advisory and Support Service to assess children's progress from emergent reader level through to Level 5. Although developed for primary use, it is useful for any students at secondary level whose reading progress needs monitoring, since it helps record what progress the student has made and helps the teacher focus on areas that need further attention. It consists of photocopiable sheets listing the attributes related to each level, on which to highlight each student's progress. Tel. 0121 428 1167 x 279.

Grammar and linguistics

- *Breakthrough to Learning, Linguistics in the service of Mainstream Education*, Mary Mason and Bob Mason. Very practical pamphlet explaining how linguistic theory can help develop language across the curriculum. Trentham Press, tel. 01782 745567.
- *The Grammar Book*, written by Richard and Elspeth Bain (1997) and produced by NATE, is widely used in secondary schools. It provides a systematic programme of activities for secondary students, founded on the premise that grammar teaching is exciting and worthwhile. A free booklet about this resource is available from 0114 255 5419.
- *Discover Grammar* David Crystal, Longman.
- *The Cheshire Cats' Guide to Grammar*. This includes useful posters and is available from Cheshire resources centre, £15, tel. 01829 74 1118; fax 01829 74 1592.
- *Grammar Guide*, Gordon Jarvie, written for professionals who don't really know any grammar. Bloomsbury, tel. 01256 302969.
- *Rediscover Grammar*, David Crystal (1998), Longman, tel. 01279 623928.

English language

- *Mother Tongue*, by Bill Bryson is very entertaining and informative reference book about the history of the English language. It contains many useful explanations of false grammatical beliefs. Published by Penguin. The supporting reference book is *Troublesome Words*, also published by Penguin.
- *The Languages Book*. A brilliant collection of material on languages, resulting from collaboration between the Institute of Education and the English and Media Centre. Full of inspiring material for lessons. English and Media Centre, tel. 020 7359 8080.

Literacy and culture

- *Amusing Ourselves to Death*, by Neil Postman, Methuen. A very interesting book on the difference television has made to a literate society.

Promoting reading and writing

- Details of a wide range of children's specialist bookshops and multicultural bookshops focusing on EAL and dual language texts are available on the National Literacy Trust's website: ww.literacytrust.org.uk/Database/childrens.html; www.literacytrust.org.uk/Database/EALres.html.
- *Boox*. Written by teenagers for teenagers, *Boox* is an excellent resource for hooking teenagers into the reading habit. Produced by Well Worth Reading, 15 Quarry Road, Winchester, Hampshire SO23 0JF; tel. 01962 865 102.
- Books and Beyond runs a readathon reading project. Contact Walsall's Learning Support Service, Education Development Centre, Pelsall Lane, Walsall WS4 1NG; tel. 01902 368 764.
- Book Trust, a charity that promotes the book, initiated the books for babies project known as Bookstart and runs Young Book Trust (YBT). It provides a wide range of publications, resources and information services, including *100 Best Books*, *The Children's Book Handbook* and a directory of authors and illustrators willing to take part in book events, *Looking for an Author?* Contact Book House, 45 East Hill, London SW18 2QZ; tel. 0181 516 2977 or Book Information Service, tel. 0181 516 2984. www.booktrust.org.uk.

- The Scottish Book Trust raises the profile of books and reading in Scotland. Contact Scottish Book Centre, 137 Dundee Street, Edinburgh EH11 1BG; tel. 0131 229 3663; e-mail: scottish.book.trust@dial.pipex.com.
- *Books for Keeps*, the children's book magazine produced by the School Bookshop Assoc. Ltd. Available on subscription £17.50 (UK) for six issues. Telephone order service: 0181 852 4953.
- Books for Students has launched *Boyz Own*, a starter reading list for boys who are reluctant or less able readers. Bird Road, Heathcote, Warwick CV34 6TB; tel. 01926 436 436.
- The British Dyslexia Association is drawing up information about dyslexia-friendly books for children. Send an s.a.e. to BDA (see page 144).
- The British Library has a diverse education programme which is free to schools and provides a free termly newsletter for teachers. Tel. 0171 412 7797 for more details, or write to 96 Euston Road, London NW1 2DB.
- Federation of Children's Book Groups is a voluntary organisation concerned with children and their books – 9 Westroyd, Pudsey, West Yorkshire, LS28 8HZ; tel. 0113 257 9950.
- NAWE – The National Association of Writers in Education, aims to represent and support writers, teachers and all those involved in the development of creative writing in education. It has a website www.nawe.co.uk which has a searchable database of writers who can go into schools. Tel/fax 01653 618429.
- The Poetry Society runs National Poetry Day (2nd Thursday in October), the Young National Poetry Competition and membership schemes for schools. Telephone 0171 420 9890, the Poetry Information Line or contact the Poetry Information Society at www.poetrysoc.com.
- *Radical Reading* is an initiative and accompanying leaflet produced by Scottish Book Trust to encourage 11–15 year olds to read with confidence. See The Scottish Book Trust above.
- Reading Is Fundamental, UK (RIF) is a National Literacy Trust project that aims to inspire children to become strong, motivated readers. RIF supports projects, and its publications include *The RIF Family Guide to Encouraging Young Readers*. Contact RIF at the National Literacy Trust (tel. 0171 828 2435).
- *Reads Like a Novel*, Daniel Pennac (1994), Quartet Books Ltd. A fascinating book about how schools tend to teach reading, but not love of reading.
- Reach produces booklists for children with reading difficulties (see special needs).
- Readathon, the sponsored national read, is now in its fourteenth year. It is often used by schools as part of National Children's Book Week. Children undertake to read books of their choice in return for pledges of money. It raises over £1 million annually to help sick children and is a proven way of stimulating children to read recreationally. Enrolled organisations receive a Readathon pack at the start of September. PO Box 89, Chipping Norton, OX7 4PR; tel. 01608 730335.
- Speaking of Books provides schools with access to leading writers, illustrators and storytellers at prices that schools can afford. They will also organise INSET days and provide book stalls. Contact Jan Powling, Speaking of Books, 9, Guildford Grove, Greenwich, London SE 10 8JY; tel/fax 0181 692 4704.

- Writers in Schools is an Arts Council project to place writers in schools. For more information contact Alison Combes, Literature Department, Arts Council of England, 14, Great Peter St London SW1P 3NQ. Tel. 0171 333 0100.

Business support

- Business in the Community – BITC's mission is to inspire business to make corporate responsibility an essential part of business excellence. Its core activities in education are literacy, numeracy, tackling underachievement and improving school management. 44 Baker Street, London W1M 1DH; tel. 0171 224 1600.
- Training and Enterprise Councils (TECs) are independent local companies led by business people working under performance-related contracts to the Government. They support schools through their Education Business Partnerships. For information about your area, tel. 01753 502370.
  (**NB** The Government's Post-16 White Paper (July 1999) proposes the abolition of TECs and the creation of a Learning Skills Council.)

Funding sources

- Education Extra funds out-of-school hours projects. It also provides resources including a *Summer Literacy Handbook* and a *Summer Literacy Resources Pack*. 17 Old Ford Road, Bethnal Green, London E2 9PL; tel. 0181 983 1061.
- Family Learning Millennium Awards, run by the Pre-school Learning Alliance and funded by the Millennium Commission, provide grants of between £1500 and £10,000 for individuals to develop family learning projects, with priority for projects involving those who are isolated or disadvantaged in some way. There are four area offices: North – 01772 423551; Central – 0121 643 0071; South West – 0117 922 1919; South East – 01732 770630.
- The Prince's Trust offers advice on setting up study support centres. 18 Park Square East, London NW1 4LH; tel. 0171 543 1234, fax 0171 543 1200.

Literacy organisations (see also special needs)

- Basic Skills Agency (BSA) is the national development agency for literacy, numeracy and related basic skills in England and Wales. It promotes, initiates and supports development of basic skills provision and resources, including a Basic Skills Quality Mark for Primary Schools and a Basic Skills Quality Mark for Secondary Schools. Contact BSA, Commonwealth House, 1–19 New Oxford Street, London WC1A 1NU; tel. 0171 405 4017, fax 0171 440 6626. Publications hotline: 0870600 2400.
- BBC Broadcast Support Service produces videos and publications on literacy and provides other learning resources. PO Box 7, London W12 8UD.
- Centre for Language in Primary Education (CLPE) is a professional development centre for teachers, providing research and publications in the area of language, literacy and assessment. Webber Row, London SE1 8QW; tel. 0171 633 0840.
- The English and Media Centre runs INSET and produces many useful publications. 18 Compton Terrace, London N1 2UN; tel. 020 7359 8080.
- NATE (National Association for the Teaching of English) is the UK subject teacher association for the teaching of English from pre-school to university. 50 Broadfield Road, Broadfield Business Centre, Sheffield S8 0XJ; tel. 0114 255 5419.

- National Literacy Association. The NLA aims to ensure that 99% of children leaving school will have adequate literacy for their needs in daily life. It runs the Docklands Learning Acceleration Project (a primary school literacy and technology project). NLA, Office no 1, the Magistrate's Court, Bargates, Christchurch, Dorset BH23 1PY; tel. 01202 484079. NLA Docklands Learning Acceleration Project, tel. 0171 537 1329
- Reading Language and Information Centre provides INSET, resources and publications on reading including pamphlets for parents. Contact University of Reading, Bulmershe Court, Earley, Reading RG6 1HY; tel. 0118 931 8820, fax 0118 931 6801.
- UKRA (United Kingdom Reading Association) is an association of teachers, educationalists and researchers of literacy and language. UKRA publishes books and runs conferences. River View, Downing Road, Whitford, Nr Holywell, CH8 9EQ, tel/fax: 01745 561959.

Volunteering organisations

- Community Service Volunteers CSV's Reading Together Scheme offers training to students in paired reading techniques to help school children aged between 7 and 12 to improve their reading and writing skills. Schools can also ask for older students to take part in the training. 237 Pentonville Road, London N1 9NJ; tel. 0171 278 6601, fax 0171 833 0149.
- Volunteer Reading Help (VRH) trains volunteers from the local community to give individual help to primary school children having difficulties in learning to read. VRH, High Holborn House, 52–54 High Holborn, London WC1V 6RL; tel. 0171 404 6204.

Resources for parents

- *Beginning with Books*, Scottish Book Trust, see above.
- *Reading Together Parents' Handbook*, Myra Barrs and Sue Ellis, Walker Books. Contact CLPE above.
- *Read and Write Together* is a magazine for parents and children aged 3–5, produced by the Basic Skills Agency and distributed to schools via LEAs.
- *Read and Write Together*. Bright and full of good ideas to encourage literacy. Available free from Broadcast Support Service, PO Box 7, London W12 8UD.
- Community Education Development Centre runs a Share Project which produces materials that provide activities for parents and children to do together. Contact CEDC, Woodway Park School, Wigston Road, Coventry CV2 2RH; tel. 01203 655700, fax 01203 655701.

Special needs

- Adult Dyslexia Organisation services include a helpline, referrals for assessment, tuition, a wide range of information and support groups. 336 Brixton Road, London SW9 7AA. Helpline 0171 924 9559; admin. 0171 737 7646. www//futurenet.co.uk/charity/ado/index.html.
- Afasic (Overcoming Speech Impairment) is a parent-led organisation that helps children and young people who have a speech and language impairment. 347 Central Markets, Smithfield, London EC1A 9NH; tel. 0171 236 3632; fax 0171 236 8115.
- BATOD (British Association of Teachers of the Deaf) represents the interests of teachers of the deaf in this country and promotes the educational interests of all hearing-impaired children, young people and adults. 41 The Orchard, Leven, Beverley, HU17 5QA; tel/fax: 01964 544 243.
- BDA (British Dyslexia Association) runs helplines, a befriender service and publishes a wide range of information to help children and adults with dyslexia. 98, London Road, Reading, RG1 5AU. Helpline 01189 668271; admin. 01189 662677.

- The Dyslexia Institute is an educational charity providing teaching, assessment, training and advice throughout the UK. 133 Gresham Road, Staines TW 18 2AJ; tel. 01784 463 851.
- National Association for Special Educational Needs aims to promote the development of children and young people with special educational needs, and support those who work with them. NASEN House, 4/5 Amber Business Village, Amber Close, Amington, Tamworth, Staffs B77 4RP; tel. 01827 311 500, fax 01827 313 005.
- National Deaf Children's Society is an organisation of families, parents and carers who work to enable deaf children to maximise their skills and abilities. 15 Dufferin Street, London EC1Y 8PD; tel. 0171 490 8656, fax 0171 251 5020, helpline 0171 250 0123.
- National Library for the Blind is a registered charity providing reading of all kinds in Braille (including music), Moon and large print (see page 00). Cromwell Road, Bredbury, Stockport SK6 2SG; tel. 0161 494 0217, fax 0161 406 6728.
- Reach – Resources for Children with Reading Difficulties provides book lists on a range of topics. Wellington House, Wellington Road, Wokingham, Berkshire RG40 2AG; tel. 0118 989 1101, fax 0118 979 0989.
- Royal National Institute for the Blind Education Support Services work with parents and professionals to improve education opportunities for visually impaired children and young people. RNIB Information Service, 224 Great Portland Street, London, WIN 6AA; tel. 0171 388 1266.
- Royal National Institute for Deaf People provides regional support groups. 19–23 Featherstone Street, London EC1Y 8SL; tel. 0171 296 8000, fax 0171 296 8199, text 0171 296 8001, helpline 0870 605 0123.
- Skill: the National Bureau for Students with Disabilities develops training and employment opportunities for young people and adults with disabilities. 336 Brixton Road, London SW9 7AA; tel. 0171 274 0565, fax 0171 264 7840.

Libraries
- School Libraries Group, part of the Library Association, provides support for the work of school librarians. SLG Secretary is Polly Smith, tel. 01928 564106.
- The School Librarian is the journal of the School Library Association. SLA, Liden Library, Barrington Close, Liden, Swindon SN3 6HF

Websites
- Basic Skills Agency, http://www.basic-skills.co.uk This useful site tells you about the range of areas that the BSA focuses on and its related publications. In particular there is information about literacy and numeracy skills in primary and secondary schools, in the adult sector and family literacy.
- BECTA – The British Educational Communications and Technology Agency website is full of useful information for teachers and parents on how to enhance learning through information technology. www.becta.org.uk
- DENI – The Department of Education In Northern Ireland's website has various sections related to literacy. http://www.nics.gov.uk/deni/index.htm
- National Association of Writers in Education website http://www.nawe.co.uk
- The National Grid for Learning is constructed as a virtual teachers' centre with information about classroom resources and professional development, as well as facilities for teachers to exchange ideas. In the primary area there is practical information about the literacy hour, as well as general information about literacy. The English sections within the secondary and special education sections focus on IT and multimedia. http://vtc.ngfl.gov.uk
- NINE, www.nine.org.uk This is Northern Ireland's virtual teacher centre – the name stands for the Northern Ireland Network for Education
- Qualifications and Curriculum Authority, www.qca.org.uk. This website covers both vocational and school-based education and assessment. The QCA contributes to the development of public policy on education and training
- SCET – The Scottish Council for Education Technology website includes a wide range of areas involving ICT and literacy. http://www.scet.com
- The Scottish Virtual Teacher Centre provides a wide range of resources and information relating to education much of which is related to literacy. www.svtc.org.uk.
- The Standards and Effectiveness Unit website includes much useful information on literacy www.standards.dfee.gov.uk
- The DfEE's Virtual Teacher Centre is full of useful resources and information, much of which relates to literacy. www.vtc.ngfl.gov.uk
- Welsh Books Council, www.cllc.org.uk. This site provides information about books in Welsh, as well as books in English with a Welsh interest, plus related material.

Family literacy

Schools wishing to establish or link up with family literacy programmes to help parents help their children will be able to find out about what programmes exist in their area by searching the database on www.literacytrust.org.uk/Database/ and a summary of approaches to family literacy on www.literacytrust.org.uk/Database/famlit, or contact the Basic Skills Agency for information on its family literacy programmes. BSA, Commonwealth House, 1–19 New Oxford Street, London WC1A 1NU; tel. 0171 405 4017, fax. 0171 404 5038. Publications hotline 0870600 2400.

If it is not here, try the National Literacy Trust's website, www.literacytrust.org.uk which has a wide range of information about hundreds of literacy organisations plus links to over 100 literacy websites.